Robert Pickering Ashe

Two kings of Uganda

Life by the shores of Victoria Nyanza

Robert Pickering Ashe

Two kings of Uganda
Life by the shores of Victoria Nyanza

ISBN/EAN: 9783337124601

Printed in Europe, USA, Canada, Australia, Japan

Cover: Foto ©Andreas Hilbeck / pixelio.de

More available books at **www.hansebooks.com**

TWO KINGS OF UGANDA;

or,

LIFE BY THE SHORES OF VICTORIA NYANZA.

BEING AN ACCOUNT OF A RESIDENCE OF SIX YEARS IN
EASTERN EQUATORIAL AFRICA.

BY

Rev. ROBERT P. ASHE, M.A., F.R.G.S., F.R.Hist.S.

NEW AND CHEAPER EDITION.

WITH MAP AND ILLUSTRATIONS.

LONDON:

SAMPSON LOW, MARSTON, SEARLE, & RIVINGTON,
LIMITED,

St. Dunstan's House,
FETTER LANE, FLEET STREET, E.C.

1890.

LONDON:
PRINTED BY WILLIAM CLOWES AND SONS, LIMITED,
STAMFORD STREET AND CHARING CROSS.

To

MY FATHER,

GEORGE ALEXANDER HAMILTON ASHE.

PREFACE TO THE SECOND EDITION.

—◆◇◆—

I HAVE taken advantage of the demand for a cheaper edition to bring the story of Uganda and its Kings up to date. Full use has been made of the important information which has come to hand during the past twelve months. To make the story compact and yet to keep the book within the limits necessary for a cheap edition, the last two chapters and the appendix, which give some account of the manners, customs, and language of the natives, have been omitted. Otherwise the book remains practically unchanged, with the exception of a very few verbal alterations. I cannot, however, allow this edition to leave my hands without speaking of one—now, alas! no more—the chief actor in many of the scenes here described, Alexander M. Mackay, who died on the 8th February, 1890, at the south of the Victoria Nyanza. How deep his loss to Africa only those who knew him well and saw his work can understand. He was one of those few who look fearlessly forth and seem to see the face of the living God. He never despaired of any person or anything. Quiet he was, and strong, and patient, and resolute, and brave; one on whom you might depend. He endured fourteen years of Africa, and what that means this book will in some measure help the reader to understand—fourteen years of the contradiction of men, black and white; fourteen years of dangers, fevers, sorrows, disappointments — and in all and through all he was steadfast, unmovable; a true missionary, always abounding in the work of the Lord.

R. P. A.

Wareham, *May*, 1890.

PREFACE.

THE events of the last few years in Eastern
Equatorial Africa have aroused so much interest in all
quarters that a book which attempts to describe them
at first hand ought not to need any apology, except on
the score of the writer's deficiencies; and of these I am
only too conscious. I should be sorry to deprecate
criticism, but it is only fair to say that the following
pages have of necessity been hastily written, amid many
interruptions, and while engaged in other work.
Indeed, they could hardly have been prepared for the
press without the kind help and encouragement I have
received on all sides.

I must first acknowledge the kindness of my old
college friend, Mr. J. Spencer Hill, of the Clarendon
Press, who has given me the greatest assistance in
reading both the MS. and the proof sheets, and has
always been ready with valuable suggestions, of which
I have largely availed myself. For the three excellent
illustrations of African scenery I have to thank the
skill of Dr. B. Woodd Walker, who drew and re-drew
them from my description, until I felt that the
impression which I myself had carried away would be
conveyed to the reader. I am indebted to the courtesy

of Mr. Eugene Stock, editorial secretary of the Church
Missionary Society, for so willingly placing at my
disposal the publications of the Society; and I must
acknowledge my obligations to Mr. Mackay and the
Rev. R. H. Walker for the free use I have made of their
correspondence. Mrs. Hannington has kindly allowed
me to reproduce a part of the Bishop's last diary; and
the Hon. Roden Noel has permitted me to insert his
lines on "Samweli" from 'A Modern Faust.' I must
also thank other friends for their willing help in
transcribing a portion of the MS. for the printers.
Lastly but not least I must acknowledge the kindness
and courtesy I have received from Mr. Marston while
the work has been in progress.

In conclusion, it may be well to explain some of the
native names which constantly occur. In the title I
have allowed the familiar word "Uganda" to remain,
though the correct form is "Buganda," which becomes
"*Uyanda*" at the coast, owing to the phonetic
interchange of "B" and "U." The root word is
"-ganda;" *Bu*ganda is the country itself, "*Mu*ganda" a
native of the country, "*Ba*ganda" the plural of
"*Mu*ganda," and "*Lu*ganda" is the language. The
same remarks apply to the interchange of "B" and
"W" so often met with—*e.g.* the "Wahuma," as Speke
names them, call themselves "Bahuma;" and I have
followed their own pronunciation, although the Baganda
call them "Bayima."

R. P. Ashe.

May, 1889.

CONTENTS.

CHAPTER I.

EN ROUTE TO MAMBOYA.

CHAPTER II.

THROUGH UGOGO TO UYUI.

CHAPTER III.

UYUI TO THE NYANZA.

CHAPTER IV.

VISIT TO ROMA AT BUZINJA.

CHAPTER V.

MUSALALA TO BUGANDA.

CHAPTER VI.

KING MUTESA.

CHAPTER VII.

INTERVIEWS WITH MUTESA.

CHAPTER VIII.

MUTESA'S DEATH.

CHAPTER IX.

THE POLITICAL CONDITION OF BUGANDA.

CHAPTER X.

ACCESSION OF MWANGA.

CHAPTER XI.

CAUSES OF SUSPICION.

CHAPTER XII.

LUGALAMA.

CHAPTER XIII.

DEATH OF LUGALAMA.

CHAPTER XIV.

INTERVIEWS WITH MWANGA.

CHAPTER XV.

NEWS OF HANNINGTON.

LIST OF ILLUSTRATIONS.

EASTERN CENTRAL AFRICA
by the
REV. R. P. ASHE. M.A. F.R.GS.

London, Sampson Low & Co, Limited.

TWO KINGS OF UGANDA.

PROLOGUE.

TWICE within the last six years it has been my lot to make my way to the shores of the Victoria Nyanza, and for a little while to turn over the pages of the book of African life as it is revealed in those regions where I sojourned, and through which I passed.

As I begin my narrative, the same feeling is uppermost in my mind as that expressed by the traveller Burton, in his book on Zanzibar, where he speaks of the sadness and solemnity of sitting down to write the story of past years.

How darkly for me the record is stained with blood —blood of the boys put to death in Uganda; of the murdered bishop who perished on the shores of the Nyanza; of the martyred natives who so nobly died; and of yet another companion, killed at Mkange, a place within sight of the coast through which my fellow-travellers and myself had passed unscathed before him, only a few weeks since, on our way to Zanzibar.

But though death has been so busy among these pioneers of Christianity and civilisation, all who have

6/

fallen have bravely done their part, and have contributed much to the great work of opening up one of the finest portions of the globe to European influence and enterprise.

I hope in the following pages to show that Africans possess the seeds of solid character, which, when developed, will enable them to overcome the destructive elements in Western civilisation. If this be so, there is no reason to despair of the future of the dark races of Africa, nor to believe that the lives which have been laid down on their behalf have been sacrificed in vain.

CHAPTER I.

EN ROUTE TO MAMBOYA.

IN May of the year 1882, a party of missionaries was on its way to various stations in the interior of East Africa, by way of Zanzibar. The journey down from Aden as a first-class passenger in the SS. *Mecca* was one of the most trying and disagreeable experiences of travel which I have ever undergone. I have dragged myself wearily over plains in Ugogo, and through the forests of Unyamwezi; I have been tossing for days on the Nyanza in native-sewn canoes; I have even been a passenger on a slave dhow upon the great lake; and I have more than once made the journey in an Arab dhow between Zanzibar and the mainland. But for thorough misery and complete discomfort, that long twelve days' struggle against the monsoon in the *Mecca* surpasses them all. As one of our passengers remarked with grim humour, we were of the number of those who say in the morning, "Would God it were even," and at even, "Would God it were morning." Overhead eternal blue sky—all around us eternal blue sea. Flying-fish were so numerous, and appeared so constantly, as to make the sight of them quite intolerable. The monotony was broken once or twice by a glimpse of Africa—now Guardafui, standing out bold and

terrible in the burning sun, making one realise vividly
the idea of

"Wild heat—raging to torture the desert."

Again, in the distance, the vague outline of the coast at
Lamu, and further to the south, Mombasa.

At length the island of Pemba came into view, and we
beheld with delight the glorious greenery of its tropical
vegetation and forgot in a moment the discomforts of
the voyage. Shortly afterwards we were within sight
of Zanzibar, where we saw in the distance the white
and dazzling buildings of the mart and capital of East
Africa. A few more hours and we were lying at anchor
opposite the Sultan's palace.

Zanzibar, or Unguja, as the natives call it, has been
so often and so admirably described that I need not
enter into any details. Had any of our party, however, possessed the poet Coleridge's faculty for counting abominable odours, he might have spent a considerable part of his time daily in doing so without
exhausting the number. In this particular Cologne
would be left far behind.

The streets of the city are narrow and tortuous, and
in the wet season are simply watercourses. A walk
through Zanzibar in a shower of rain is quite an adventure; overhead water is pouring off the flat roofs in
cataracts, while underfoot is a swiftly-flowing torrent
ankle deep. In fine weather, however, the whole town
is alive with bustle and business, and bright with the
variegated costumes of many nations. Shops there are

of all kinds and descriptions, kept by all manner of people. Fair-faced languid-looking Indian women sit and display their wares, waiting patiently for customers, as also men of the same nation, who, to judge by their appearance, have evidently grown fat upon their gains ; their commodities include cotton-stuffs, spices, gold and silver thread, lamps, attar of roses, onions, and other miscellaneous articles of frequent barter. Fruit-shops too abound, kept by vivacious negroes; there are also not a few almost European establishments owned by Goanese, where anything in reason may be purchased, from a dress-suit to a packet of pins. Arabs are stalking along with an air of superb contempt—the Arab has certainly mastered the art of looking as if the place belongs to him. Here comes one of them riding a gaily-caparisoned donkey, his slaves running in front calling out, "simila, simila," "by your leave." Now we meet a big black man carrying two enormous bunches of bananas slung over his shoulder at each end of a stick, he also cries out "simila." At another place a bevy of women and girls, every one of them slaves, are at work carrying mortar and stones for the masons who are building a neighbouring house, all the while chanting some monotonous but not unmusical African melody. Further on a number of men chained together are at work. They are the Sultan's chain-gang undergoing penal servitude for offences against his Highness, or at the instance of some one of the European consuls. One day I encountered the Sultan's soldiers in a narrow street; to my surprise they politely broke their ranks to let me pass. The army is, on the whole, well-drilled, and, could the men be depended upon to obey a European, they would be formidable antagonists to any opposing native force on the mainland.

It had been arranged that we should take up our quarters at the French hotel. I was invited, however, to be the guest of the Universities Mission at Mbweni, a beautiful place some four miles out of the town, where there is a large and flourishing training establishment for freed slave-girls. There were many wonderful things at Mbweni, including among others a steam-roller; but what struck me most was a novel kind of razor in use among the girls, which consisted of a piece of broken glass with a chisel-shaped edge. I have never seen this substitute for a razor anywhere, although shaving the head is a universal custom among Africans.

After nine days of preparation, we found ourselves on board an Arab dhow bound for the mainland, with a fair breeze behind us. The dhow was a dirty and dingy craft, some forty feet long by nine feet beam. She had no deck, and so we were obliged to perch ourselves unhappily here and there on the top of boxes. When we neared Sadaani the tide was out and our vessel stuck fast some quarter of a mile from the beach, bumping heavily on the bottom as every wave rolled under her. This must have been most damaging to the dhow, it certainly was exceedingly unpleasant for her passengers. We were not, however, long left in this situation. A miserable dug·out canoe half-filled with water came alongside to take us ashore. And so at last, as the sun was going down, our little company stood safe and sound on African soil.

It is needless to dwell much upon the details of our outfit, but I may mention some of the mistakes which were made : we were provided with Epsom salts by the stone, but found ourselves short of common table salt. Our large supply of castor oil was but a poor compensation for the entire absence of such a necessary as butter, and for my part I would gladly have exchanged our elaborate distilling apparatus for another common tea-kettle. The ordinary equipment of an African traveller consists of tents, camp-beds, chairs, stools, buckets, pots, pans, cups and saucers, plates, blankets, guns, pistols, boxes of clothes and books, scientific instruments, provisions and medicines. He carries with him also goods for barter, consisting of bales of cloth made up into loads of from sixty to seventy pounds; beads of various kinds, copper, brass and iron wire, gunpowder, and soap, which is a very important article of commerce in the interior.

Our caravan was made up of nearly five hundred porters, or Wapagazi, as they are called—none too many for a large party of seven white men, a greater number of Europeans than is usually seen together in Central Africa. Our leader was Mr. Charles Stokes, who had already made the journey to Uganda; the others were the Revs. James Hannington (the future first Bishop of Eastern Equatorial Africa), Cyril Gordon, Joseph Blackburn, Walter Edmonds, Mr. Wise and myself.

Each of us had engaged one or more Zanzibar or Freretown mission boys as personal servants. My boy, Tom Tofiki, was quite above the average, and possessed, at any rate, the great virtue of honesty; he was somewhat sluggish and by no means a good walker or worker —in fact he either would not or could not do anything very well except sing hymns, and that he did excellently. He never learnt to cook anything except "ugali," a thick coarse kind of porridge, and he used every morning to concoct a peculiar compound which he called coffee, but which rather exercised one's faith when it appeared at breakfast.

Our other porters were distributed in three camps: the Wangwana or Zanzibaris, who were all nominally Mahometans; the Wanyamwezi, whose country stretches from the other side of Ugogo to the Nyanza, and the Wasukuma, or people of the north, who live on the shores of the lake. The Wangwana individually often display many fine and admirable qualities, though in large numbers they generally give infinite trouble. My experience with them on the whole has been fortunate, and I rarely found them insubordinate without some apparent reason for their disobedience. The Wanyamwezi belong to a sturdy and enterprising race; they come in great numbers to the coast, conducting their own caravans. I have often seen four or five hundred of these

people travelling entirely on their own account, bringing
the ivory belonging to their principal chiefs to the coast
for sale. It is curious that the Wagogo, whose country
lies between the Wanyamwezi and the sea, rarely or
never venture to Zanzibar themselves, but are content
to make the Wanyamwezi pay toll for passing through
their territory, both going and returning. The Wasukuma, or Northerners (which the name implies), who
live on the south and south-east shore of the Nyanza,
are in many respects similar to the Wanyamwezi, but
are even less civilised. In their own country the men,
at any rate, entirely dispense with clothing; but at
the coast they give way somewhat to the prejudices of
civilisation. All the porters, whether from Zanzibar or
from the interior, are divided into small companies
under head men, at the coast called "Wazee," or elders,
by the Wanyamwezi, "Wanamhara" or "Wanyampara,"
which has the same meaning. It is an almost universal
custom for people from the interior to take a new
name when they reach Zanzibar. Mahometan names
are often chosen, such as Hamisi, Omali, Tofiki, and
the like.

After a couple of days at Sadaani we began our long
march into the interior. Of this town I need say
little: it is a mongrel and miserable place, partly
Arabian, partly Indian, and wholly African. We were
courteously received by Bwana Heri, its governor, who
finds it to his interest to keep on good terms with
Europeans. Soon after leaving the town we entered

on a beaten track or footpath some eighteen inches or two feet wide. Footpaths of this kind wind on from village to village, and connect tribe with tribe, so that the traveller finds the way clearly marked and well defined throughout the whole of this wide region.

The first few marches were not examples of successful African travelling; frequently we were up and off without anything to eat; often we had to wait for hours after reaching our camp until our tents came up, and before the cooks could prepare any kind of a dinner another couple of hours had usually passed away. On one occasion we were twenty-four hours without a meal—a specimen of the blunders which inexperienced travellers make, and sometimes with fatal results, of which the African climate is made to bear the blame, rather than the travellers' carelessness. Nor did matters seem to improve as we advanced, the fact being that there were far too many of us for comfortable travelling. While making the first stage of our journey through Useguha, we were fairly well supplied with native food —unripe bananas boiled and mashed, beans, sweet potatoes, rice, and the invariable fowls and goats. One day, while enjoying this fare in our dining-tent, we saw to our consternation that the grass to leeward* of us had been set alight by the natives, and soon a glorious line of fire came sweeping up towards where we were

---

* I believe it to be a fact, that except in case of a very high wind, an African prairie fire will come up against the breeze rather than with it as might be expected.

encamped. Immediately our men rushed out pell-mell to meet it, armed with boughs and sticks, and after an exciting contest succeeded in beating it down. Soon afterwards, while we were finishing our dinner, we saw all the men rushing madly off in the direction of the villages, yelling and brandishing their spears and other weapons, intent on taking revenge upon the natives, who had twice this day fired the grass in the neighbourhood of our camp. Stokes dashed after them, calling out as he passed, "Gentlemen, my men are off, and I cannot stop them; you may write that in your books." Alas, how often has the African traveller to write in his journal that his men have bolted; he is only fortunate if they do not take some of his valuables with them. I think our porters reckoned on the support both moral and physical of the white men; but when they saw that we were determined to prevent their attacking the natives, they obeyed their head men and came quietly back, and so ended what to us had been a very exciting day. We travelled on slowly, passing by the hills of Enguru to the beautiful mountain region of Mamboya, which is the first English mission station on this route. It is situated on the side of a lofty hill, which rises far above it; and, standing on the verandah of the house, we looked sheer down into a circular valley enclosed by a glorious panorama of mountains, which tower one above another, and stretch away mountain beyond mountain until they lose themselves in the blue distance.

CHAPTER II.

RELUCTANTLY we left Mamboya and turned our faces westward once more; the road here winds along the rocky mountains which stretch for fifty miles up to Mpwapwa or Mhamva, on the borders of the Malenga Makali, the "wilderness of bitter waters." This road is proverbially dangerous, being infested by the Rugaruga, or fighting men of the Wahehe tribe. The danger is no imaginary one, as I know by experience, for in the year 1886 I sent one of my men this way with a message, when he was badly wounded, and a Munyamwezi man who was with him was shot dead. The last time that I passed through the same district I myself saw the naked body of a poor lad, doubtless some straggler from a passing caravan, lying dead at the side of the path, pierced by many spear wounds. It is not surprising, therefore, that our party should encounter these notable Ruga-ruga. About a dozen of them showed themselves to our advanced guard; but when they saw white men armed with guns, they made a precipitate retreat, their flight accelerated by a volley from the guns of the Europeans. I was behind at the time and did not share in this victory. One of our party, however, very nearly lost his life, for during the encounter, his neighbour's gun went off by accident and shot the sight off the rifle which he was holding, but fortunately did no further damage.

The Malenga Makali, or Wilderness of Chunyo, is so called from the strong saline water found at both sides of it, which is especially strong in Ugogo. We made our camp at the entrance of this waterless tract; but before undertaking the next stage of our journey, we visited the beautiful mission station of Kisokwe. There we stayed till late, talking with our hospitable hosts, Mr. and Mrs. Cole, for we knew that we should be able to make our way to our camp by moonlight. At midnight, when we reached the wind-swept plain in which our tents had been pitched, we found that they had been blown down. We shouted in vain for our boys. At last we began pulling the tent about, intending to set it up ourselves. A deep and sleepy groan issued from the tangled heap of canvas and ropes, and out crept our boys Tom and Robert, the youths whose duty it was to have had the tent ready for our reception. This little incident is an admirable illustration of African character. Sooner than take the very small amount of trouble involved in tightening the ropes and hammering in the pegs, they preferred to let the tent collapse entirely. The expression " Haithuru," the Irishman's " Och, it'll do," is the formula with which both Celt and Swahili leave undone, with an untroubled conscience, any necessary but distasteful duty.

The next afternoon we entered the wilderness and

kept on until nightfall, when we waited an hour or two for the appearing of the moon, by the light of which we intended to continue our journey. In a few minutes the prairie, which but an hour before had been loneliness itself, the silence only broken by the incessant chirping of the grass crickets, or the call of some night-bird, or the weird, dismal howling of the hyænas, was suddenly blazing with a hundred fires, and loud with the crackling of dry fuel, and the laughter and ceaseless chatter of our five hundred porters. A few hours later solitude again resumed her reign, and the scene relapsed into the silence from which it had been so strangely awakened. Wearied with our long night march, we were glad indeed as the dawn broke to find ourselves entering upon Ugogo.

Ugogo is a succession of great bare plains, enclosed by hills, rising abruptly from the level of the plain, which is studded here and there with the enormous baobab or "embuyu" trees, and at frequent intervals the small villages or "tembes" of the people. These are long, narrow, low, mud-roofed buildings forming an enclosed square, into the centre of which the cattle are driven at night. A "tembe" may contain from two to twenty families, according to its size. The architecture of Ugogo is the poorest attempt at house-building I have ever met with, except the grass huts of the handsome Watusi or Wahuma herdsmen.

The Wagogo, like the Masai have large herds of cattle, but they cultivate the ground extensively, while the latter do not. I imagine that they are very closely allied to the Masai tribe; for their weapons are much the same, and it is a moot point whether the Masai supply the Wagogo with the great broad-bladed spears they use, or *vice versâ.* The Wagogo warriors are a wild-looking set with their great spears and painted shields. Their dress consists of a bib of leather, not reaching quite to the waist; a small square of leather hangs behind, and serves as a mat to sit upon; a thong of hide round the waist, falling down at one side or behind, giving them the appearance of possessing a tail. They twist string of their own manufacture into their short woolly hair, and the ends hang down to their shoulders like long plaited hair. Both men and women frightfully distend the lobes of their ears, and the women insert a piece of wood which looks like a large-sized "draughtsman." The pear-shaped end of a bottle-gourd is also a usual ornament for the ears of both sexes, as well as other miscellaneous articles; I have seen, for instance, a husk of Indian corn, a snuff-box, the handle of a teacup, an empty cartridge-case, and a bishop belonging to a set of chessmen, fulfilling this duty of ear-distender. Our party was a source of continual wonder to these unsophisticated people. I recollect one day, when separated from my companions, being found by a group of Wagogo. I was evidently a new sort of man, and the first specimen of the kind which they had ever seen. Their astonishment knew no bounds. One old man ventured to approach while I stood still for inspection; he cautiously advanced one finger till it touched my beard, and then timidly withdrew it. The next thing which attracted his attention was my ear; he again put out his hand and very gently took hold of it, feeling it to see what it was made of, but I had no time to spare them for more minute examination.

Water was always a difficulty in Ugogo, and at one camp it was so bad as to be, I should think, poisonous; it did not lose its horrible stench even when made into strong coffee. It was here that one of our companions, Hannington, became so ill that we almost despaired of his life. In fact he sent for us to say farewell. We revived him, however, with stimulants, and in a day or two more he was able to be carried forward.

We passed out of Ugogo into the great wilderness called the " Mugunda Mukali," which separates Ugogo and Unyamwezi. This Mugunda Mukali, "or terrible garden," takes at least six days to pass through, and food has to be carried to last during that time. Our porters bought their meal, and, wrapping it in a piece of calico, slung it round their waists; this, and the calabash for water and the cooking-pot which every fifth or sixth man carried, completed their outfit. The dreaded banditti, or Ruga-ruga, also infest this wilderness, and it was while journeying here that a young Englishman named Penrose lost his life some years before. He had been sent out by the Church Missionary Society, and was

bringing up a caravan from the coast. A chief named
Nyungu, whose villages lay at some distance from the
caravan route, had recently quarrelled with a French
traveller, the Abbé du Bayx. The Frenchman had a
powerful and well-armed caravan, and the chief was
afraid to attack him; but he vowed vengeance against
the next white man who passed that way, and this
happened to be young Penrose. He was deserted by
his men, who carried off his ammunition in their flight,
and, though he stood his ground, he fell at last
overpowered by numbers. This encounter took place
by the banks of a small lake called Chaya. Some
time afterwards, our leader Stokes passed the place, and
among the skulls which were lying about picked out
one which from its conformation seemed to be that of
a European, and buried it. We emerged from the
Mugunda Mukali with a great firing of guns and
rejoicing on the part of our porters at having come in
safety through the "terrible garden." We spent a day or
two at a place called Itura, and then once more entered
a wilderness, which stretches some sixty miles up to
Uyui, the second stage of our journey. Here, while
making a night march, we came suddenly upon a lion
at his supper. We had left our camp at midnight with
about twenty porters, as there was a glorious moon.
Stokes, with the main body, was to follow the next
day. Hannington and I were behind, and he was
propounding the question "who was the prophetess
Noadiah." However, the sudden crack of a rifle a few

c

hundred yards ahead, followed by a sustained fusillade, rudely dismissed Noadiah from our thoughts, and concluding that it must be an attack of the ubiquitous Ruga-ruga, we rushed to the front, where we found a scene of great confusion. Many of the party were scrambling up a tree, loads were lying about in all directions, some of the men were holding their emptied smoking guns, a fine retriever dog which we had with us was barking furiously; and all this commotion was caused by the royal diner-out, no doubt annoyed at being so unceremoniously disturbed. Hannington in a state of great excitement seized his fowling-piece; Tom handed me my pistol which he was carrying, and Gordon grasping his umbrella, we advanced to the attack. Hannington's guardian angel, in the shape of one of the porters, now rushed forward, imploring him not to imperil his life, and to emphasise his appeal he hung on to his master's coat-tails. Hannington sent his would-be deliverer reeling backwards; but during this little diversion, one of my tent-boys, Robert, rushed past us with a small rifle which he had borrowed from one of our companions, and wildly let fly, as quickly retreating again. The lion now drew off further into the jungle, where we could still hear his angry growling. Then came a struggle in Hannington's mind, between his passion for adventure and more prudential considerations; but I think we all felt that it was hardly worth while to run the risk for no particular purpose of receiving the attack of a wounded lion—we could not hope at the first shot to do more than disable him, since it was too dark to see anything, and besides we were insufficiently armed, and therefore we turned tail and left him master of the field. Our porters, seeing that the attack was abandoned, now descended from their tree, and once more we resumed our journey, but not till late the next day did we reach Uyui.

Here Hannington became so desperately ill, that we decided it was impossible for him to attempt the journey to the Nyanza in his present state. We could not keep our large caravan waiting indefinitely, and so, after remaining twelve days, in hopes some decided improvement might take place, we were obliged to resume our journey without him. This anxious time at Uyui I shall never forget. Until I left, I took it in turns with Gordon to watch by our sick friend. He was lying in a large, bare room without any door, the only furniture being a camp-bed and a few boxes. He was often delirious with fever, and as night drew on his brain would become full of the busy fancies which fever brings. In that dimly-lighted room the shadow of death seemed to be almost visibly hovering. Without, ever and anon, one could hear the dismal howling of the hyenas which were skulking round the house. Within, the sick man kept on uttering what seemed ever uppermost in his mind, the word "Uganda" constantly recurring. Suddenly he called out, "He has come!" "Who has come," I said. "Mackay has

c 2

come to meet me, and has brought it." "What has he brought?" I soothingly asked. "A coffin," he replied, and turned over in his troubled sleep only to dream again of something terrible; and so the long night wore away.

CHAPTER III.

At Uyui we bade our companions farewell, and, with our number now reduced by one-half, we struck due north along the route which Stanley had taken when he crossed the Continent. Passing by a very friendly chief called Mutinginya, we were stopped at a little village in his neighbourhood, where the people wished to levy "hongo," or the usual blackmail; and on our refusing to pay their demands, they forbade our men to draw water, and stationed an armed guard round the well during the night. Next day our people were determined to go and take the water by force, and it was with no little difficulty we prevented bloodshed. However, our friend Mutinginya, on being appealed to, sent over one of his Wanhamhara, "head men," who settled the matter satisfactorily; and we were allowed to go peaceably on our way.

At one of the villages in the neighbourhood I witnessed for the first time the extraordinary body-dance which prevails among so many African tribes. It consists of a rhythmical contortion of the whole of the body, the shoulders and breast and stomach being twisted and worked about in all directions. The first time you see it, it looks a most disgusting and degrading exhibition; but in time one gets used to the sight. On this occasion it was performed by a number of young girls, who worked themselves up into an extraordinary state of excitement, and looked as if they were under the influence of some magician's spell. They gradually approach a stranger nearer and nearer, advancing slowly till they touch him with their hands. In my case, I broke the charm by giving them some beads, which sent them away quite satisfied, and left me even more pleased at their departure.

We now entered the Manonga " pori," or desert. A long tramp of eighteen miles brought us to the Manonga River, which some of our men told me was " mto mkubwa sana," " a very big river." I saw a fringe of tall trees—the invariable sign of a river—but on reaching the bank and looking down no water was visible. To adapt Hood—

> " I saw instead but the river bed,
> For the faithless stream was dry."

However, by digging about a foot we came to fairly good water. It is a common circumstance with many African rivers in the dry season to sink beneath the sand, though it gives the inexperienced traveller considerable disappointment.

Our next adventure was with the hostile natives of Samwè—the nearest inhabited district—with whom we had a long four-days' palaver, or " shauri," about the payment of hongo. In fact, things came to such a pass that the natives determined to fight. They brought out their flag and defiantly planted it outside the village. The women were ordered inside the stockade, and soon the great war drum rolled out its summons to the warriors of neighbouring villages to come to the attack. Upon this we yielded, and paid their enormous demand of more than a thousand yards of white cotton cloth ; but we said, " We will not go further this way, but will return straight back by the way we have come." " You may go where you like," they insolently replied, " now that you have paid." However, when we actually did go back—which they did not believe we should do—they sent messengers after us to beg us to return, and offered to restore the cloth which they had extorted from us ; but we were firm. We had been promised another road by the great chief Mirambo, who wished to have Europeans in his country ; so we determined to go to him and claim his promise. I may say that eventually, through Mutinginya's influence, we regained most of the cloth which the people of Samwè had made us pay, and six cows for the bale which they had already cut up. The cows we presented to Mutinginya as an acknowledgment of all the trouble he had taken on our behalf.

The news of our return had preceded us to Uyui, where we had left Hannington ill, with Gordon, who was especially taking care of him. Such an unexpected event electrified him into new life, and in spite of his great weakness and the intense suffering which he had already undergone, he formed the heroic resolution of pushing on to the Nyanza.

It is needless to enter into details of this trouble-some journey, yet it must not be supposed that moving about in any part of East Africa is free from difficulty. It is a long series of worries, greater or less, and fever and fatigue are almost necessary accompaniments.

Five or six days' travelling brought us into the country of the great chief Mirambo, who has been called, not inaptly, the Napoleon of East Africa. In the beginning of his career he was only a small "Munhamhara," or head man; but by his genius and force of character he gradually consolidated his power, and made himself master of nearly the whole of Unyamwezi. Marvellous for the rapidity of his marches and the suddenness of his attacks, his name at this time was a terror to his enemies, and, as we had occasion to prove more than once, a tower of strength to his friends. I have read somewhere that the name "Mirambo" has an etymological connection with killing people: it may be something more than a coincidence that in the Luganda language the word "mirambo" means "corpses."

Some of us paid this redoubted chieftain a visit at his "Gwikuru," or capital, where I saw, to my astonish-ment, a large four-sided house, built after the manner of Zanzibar. It was by far the most solid structure I have ever seen in the interior of Africa. A number of Zanzibar masons and carpenters, "mafundi," were employed upon it. Mirambo received us courteously in a small circular hut which he used as a general reception-room for his guests, and where he transacted business. The walls were lined with quivers full of poisoned arrows. The chief was dressed in a short English-made coat and the customary native loin-cloth, but the material was richer than that usually worn. He was a tall, fine-looking man, with a good, clever face. After ordering his attendants to bring us stools to sit upon and a large calabash of fresh milk, the conversation began—through an interpreter, of course. He asked us where we were going, and when he understood it was to Uganda, he said, " Ah, truly your beards will have grown long e'er you return." What else we discoursed of I cannot recall ; but after talking for about half an hour, and renewing his promise of protection and help, he bade us farewell.

The contrast between Mirambo and Mutesa—the two greatest chiefs whom I met with during my sojourn in Central Africa—was most striking in every particular. Mirambo, kindly and courteous to all, frank and friendly with strangers, living as a plain man among his fellows, although so much greater than they in all that makes men great. Mutesa, kindly too, but formal, fearful of his dignity, crafty, suspicious, and capable of acts so vile and foul that they may only be hinted at, surrounded by an abject court, an object of grovelling adoration to slavish thousands, but really great in nothing. This is the Mutesa of whom, later on, I have more to say.

The very name of Mirambo inspired so much fear in the breasts of our Moslem porters that they had deserted us by dozens. Mirambo had been carrying on a constant war with the Arabs at Unyanyembe, their important trading centre, which was in his country, and many Arabs and their black Mahometan slaves and retainers had fallen in the frequent encounters which had taken place. Hence the dislike of their co-religionists in our caravan to put themselves in the power of the chief. Their fear was altogether imaginary, for Mirambo never would have touched one of them, at any rate while with a European.

Another fortnight's journey through the picturesque district of Musalala brought us to the Nyanza, or at least to one of the swamps in which a small arm of the mighty lake terminates. Passing through the villages of this district, I saw for the first time a native loom at work. The spinning of the cotton is carried on in the spare moments of some of the youths. The apparatus is very simple : a stick with a hook at one end, and just below the hook a round disk through which the stick passes ; to get the twist the cotton is rubbed with the palm of the hand on the naked thigh of the spinner, just as the cobbler at home twists his wax end. The loom is of the roughest construction. The shuttle is slowly passed through the threads by the fingers of the weaver; and I think it takes fully three months to finish a piece of cloth two or three yards in length. When finished it is very strong, and has a dark-coloured border woven in; the yarn for the border is dyed in a peculiar manner. This cloth is largely worn by the women of Unyamwezi.

Here too I saw for the first time native Africans at work forging iron. Large quantities of wood are collected and burned into charcoal, but no oven of any kind is used. The smithies are grass huts erected over a convenient boulder or out-cropping rock. This forms the anvil, and for a hammer a large round stone is used; but in Buganda the people manufacture their hammers of iron. The ore is smelted in a charcoal furnace, the blast for which is supplied by bellows made out of goat-skin, tied on a piece of hollowed cup-shaped wood; there is no valve, but a space is left between the clay tube which conducts the blast to the furnace and the aperture in the wooden cup; the bellows are worked up and down by a vertical stick, round which the skin is gathered in the centre.

It was with the most eager anxiety that we awaited our first view of the great Nyanza, to reach which we had undergone so many toils and such utter weariness. We had visions of looking out upon a vast expanse of sparkling sapphire, and could already hear in imagination the breaking of the waves upon the beach. When the final march of twenty miles was over and we reached the last village before the lake, we felt sure that we should get a grand view of the water; but all we saw was a scrubby bit of forest. Before we rested we set off to seek for the Nyanza; after walking about three miles we came to a piece of rising ground, and following with our eyes the direction indicated by one of the elders of the village who had accompanied us, we saw in the valley below a long strip of vividly green grass and nothing more. "That," said our imperturbable guide, "is the Nyanza." It was with much disappointment that we retraced our steps, and it was not for another month that we really did see the never-to-be-forgotten sight of the illimitable expanse of that glorious inland ocean.

CHAPTER IV.

VISIT TO ROMA AT BUZINJA.

WHILE at the far end of the creek marked "Smith's Sound" on the map, we were in the territory of a young chief named Sonda, with whom we left most of our property. We pitched our tents in the forest some little distance apart, and about a mile from the village. We piled up thorn bushes to keep off wild beasts, and the first night that I spent in this forest I happened to be by myself. I had allowed my two boys to sleep in the village, as they had not finished building their huts near me. Before they left they had made a large fire in front of the tent, a welcome luxury on those chilly evenings. When their cheery "Kwa-heri, bwana," "Good-night, sir," died away, I was alone. A feeling of the utter strangeness of my position stole over me. Can it be true that I am in an African forest a thousand miles away from even the outskirts of civilisation? It is at such a time as this that the unanswerable problem of human life forces itself upon the mind, and the absorbing questions, What am I? Whence came I? Whither am I going? Why am I here? present themselves with overwhelming power. Those who know something of the "blank misgivings of a creature moving about in worlds not realised" will be able to sympathise with the feelings of one placed for the first time in the midst of this great unknown, unrealised world of strange, mysterious Africa. I was, however, startled from my musings by hearing the deep roar of a lion close at hand; but he moved off in another direction, and his voice became fainter and fainter, until at last it died away in the distance.

Our days while we sojourned here were spent in sickness and other employments, as one writer of African experiences has put it with unconscious humour. The other employments in our case were superintending the building of our temporary houses, buying, selling, cooking, writing letters. It was during this time that Hannington met with one of the most extraordinary lion adventures on record. He had gone out with his gun, followed by his servant boy Bakiti, when he saw a small animal at some distance moving in the long grass. He had no suspicion what it was; he raised his gun and fired, and the little creature rolled over dead. Instantly, with a terrific roar, there sprang out two great full-grown lions and came bounding towards him. His gun was empty, there was no time even to reload, so he turned and ran. The lions were almost upon him, and as his pace grew slower and more uncertain, he heard the agonised cry of his faithful Bakiti, " Hapana, hapana, kimbia!" " No, no, run!" urging him to swifter flight. He, however, translated it " Don't, don't run," and immediately faced round. The lions then stood still, waving their tails and glaring at their strange opponent. It was an awful moment. At last the divinity which hedges the courageous conquered the lions, and they crept away abashed. Now it was Hannington's turn to be the pursuer, so waving his arms and shouting, he drove them away, and actually carried off the dead carcase of the fallen whelp.

Christmas was now drawing on, and although we were all of us more or less ill with fever and ague, we determined not to be done out of our Christmas dinner. Hannington has humorously described my pudding with its weevily flour and fermented raisins, but these drawbacks were in some degree counterbalanced by fresh eggs and good currants and suet and native meal. At any rate it was a great treat, and a Christmas feast of plum pudding is a national custom which every Englishman likes to observe.

While we were at Musalala, Roma, King of Buzinja, a country on the south-west of the Nyanza, sent messengers and presents inviting us to visit him and promising to provide canoes to take us on to Uganda. Hannington thought it best to accept his offer, and as we were dissatisfied with our present situation, it was arranged that I should go with him and Gordon to Roma's capital to look out for a suitable site near the lake for the new station at the south of the Nyanza: and that Wise should stay behind to look after the camp.

The journey to Roma's took us quite nine days, and

a very trying and disagreeable time it was. Our bill
of health was anything but satisfactory. Gordon was
so ill that he could not stand, and had to be carried;
Hannington was only just able to crawl, while I was
on the verge of a bad attack of fever, and altogether,
our experiences during this voyage, with drunken,
insubordinate and quarrelsome canoemen, in leaky
canoes, with insufficient provisions, and sometimes no
shelter, were not encouraging. One night we were
landed on a desolate shore in pouring rain and pitch
darkness, and after floundering miserably for about a
mile through grass dripping wet, and stumbling over
scattered rocks, we came to some human habitations,
and begged the owners for a night's lodging. They
said they were sorry, but they had nothing to offer
except a goat-house. We went to see it; but we
could not venture into such a filthy place. As the
rain had now ceased, we made our damp beds in the
little courtyard, and tried to sleep, but in vain; for
the rain came on again faster than ever. Here let me
record an act of rare kindness, one out of kindnesses
innumerable received from Africans. The good people
of the house, when they saw our sorry plight, took
compassion on us, and actually turned out of their
warm, snug dwelling to make room for us, while
they themselves spent the night huddled together under
a rough thatched shed outside.

We reached Roma's headquarters at last, all very
weak, and so ill that we had to stay in bed. Our beds

occupied the three sides of one not very large tent.
Hannington, who found adventures in all places,
beguiled the time in the intervals of fever with
yachting recollections or reminiscences of cliff-climbing
in Devonshire. We soon had a visit from the chief,
a man of gigantic stature, partly sprung from the
Bahuma race; but his good traits were. sadly spoilt
by cowardice, suspicion, and conceit; and no ancient
Highland crone could be more superstitious than this
representative of African royalty.

We had not been long, however, with Roma before
we discovered that he had simply brought us into a
trap. He made some paltry excuse for refusing us
canoes, and extorted a large present; and to comply with
his demands we had to encroach grievously upon our
rapidly diminishing store of cloth. After much diplomatic intercourse the chief allowed Hannington to
leave for Kageye, on the other side of Smith's Sound.
We decided before he left that if he were successful
in procuring canoes, he should send them for us, and
that to induce Roma to let us go quickly, we would give
him some of the small breech-loading guns which our
porters were carrying. There are possibly some who
may blame missionaries for giving a heathen chief fire-
arms under any circumstances; but they belong to
that select class who are given to fault-finding.
But in our favour it should be remembered that we
were short of cloth with which to buy even necessary
food, and that as we had but little ammunition to give

D

with the guns, they were not likely to do much harm.
The question, however, is perhaps a fair one as to how
far the Christian Church is justified, in the first instance, in sending missionaries to countries which they
cannot reach without being armed.

Hannington succeeded in despatching canoes to take
us away, and while Gordon looked after the baggage, I
took the three little guns to give them to Roma. I
was invited into the straw-built house in which the
king received his chiefs and visitors, and duly presented our offering. In showing him how to load one of
the rifles, I happened, before inserting the cartridge,
to point the gun at my host. He nervously put it to
one side with his hand, and I could not help smiling
at his apprehension; this he evidently noticed, and so
he gravely took the carbine from me, and deliberately
loaded it and pointed it full at my breast. It was
my turn now to be dismayed, and I quickly put aside
the muzzle as he had done, saying at the same time,
" Poli, poli ! " " Gently, gently ! " This was just what
he wanted. " Poli, poli, is it ? " he cried ; " O ho ! so the
Muzungu (white man) does not like a gun pointed at
him." And the old fellow shook with laughter,
repeating the words " poli," " poli," between his bursts
of merriment.

He and I had had a passage of arms some days
before this, when he had come to see us. On that
occasion he said very rudely to me that I was only a
child. " How then do you account for my beard ? " I

MULESHI'S FERRY.   SOUTH END OF VICTORIA NYANZA.

To face p. 35.

asked. "Very easily," he replied, "you were born with it." I could only make the rather weak and obvious retort that his not having a beard proved him to be a child—a retort which did not altogether please him.

Roma dismissed us kindly, and we managed to place all the baggage on board the canoes, and then Gordon and I took our seats. The canoemen, however, flatly refused to stir; they said that we should all be drowned, and that the canoes were overloaded. This latter statement was undoubtedly true; but what else could we do but make a start? However, when we urged them to go, they remained resolute in their refusal, and so I had to get out again with my eight men, and we decided that I should do the journey on foot back to Wise, whom we had left at Musalala, and that Gordon should join Hannington at Kageye.

Soon after I had made my way down to Musalala on the west of Smith's Sound, Hannington walked into our camp, having come down on the east side and crossed over at Muleshi's ferry. He was in a very serious condition. He had had so many repeated attacks of fever, and had suffered so much, that he at last felt that he was not justified in resisting our urgent advice that he should endeavour to reach the coast.

When all was ready for the start, I accompanied him for a mile or so of the way, and then sorrowfully we said farewell and clasped hands for the last time. I stood and my eyes followed the tall receding figure, now indeed bowed with the intense pain and suffering which he had undergone, and I wondered, as I watched him, whether he would ever accomplish the long eight hundred miles of swamp and wilderness, with its certain toils and unknown perils, which lay between him and Zanzibar.

CHAPTER V.

AFTER making the young chief Sonda an "appropriate" and suitable present of a pair of trousers, a tin box, and a surplice, Wise and I left Musalala, and started for Kageye. When we had reached the other side of the Urima creek, we received letters with the news that a small caravan of cloth was on its way to join us at Musalala. Wise very kindly offered to go back to meet it, while I hastened on to join Gordon at Kageye. The people of Urima are not unlike the Wanyamwezi, except that they do not chip the triangular gap in their two front teeth, and the men have even less idea of decency in the matter of clothing; the women, however, are dressed in skins. The curiosity we excited was unbounded. It was quite common for a bevy of women and girls to cluster thickly round our tent, making remarks and laughing at everything they saw. On one occasion I went to the door of the tent and offered some half-pence, hoping to propitiate these dark damsels. They, however, misunderstood my charitable intentions and there was a general stampede. I could not help laughing immoderately on seeing one huge creature fall heavily in her eager anxiety to make good her escape. A minute afterwards they

were all back again as talkative as ever. This went on
all day, except sometimes boys and youths took the
places of the women and girls. Our male visitors were
more bumptious, ignorant, and conceited than those of
the other sex, and were some of the most objectionable
persons I have ever met with.

We were now travelling in the rains, and our road lay
chiefly through morass and swamp. We had to pass
through a district called Usmawo, famous for the avarice
and turbulence of its people. Usmawo lies midway
between the districts of Urima and Usukuma, from
which latter place we had engaged a number of naked
savages as porters. Owing to the bad character of the
people through whose country we were about to travel,
we decided to make the attempt to slip past them in the
night. Just as the sun went down we left our camp,
and cautiously the thin line of dusky figures crept
onwards through the darkness. Some of the long
black trunks, carried by the unclad Wasukuma porters,
looked like coffins in the dim light, and the moonbeams
gleaming on the white paint of others gave them from
a little distance the appearance of pale and flickering
fires; and so in solemn silence this ghostly band
of naked figures filed past the sleeping villages of
Usmawo like a procession of the dead. To our great
satisfaction we reached the border unobserved, but
immediately we crossed over and stood in the territory of the Wasukuma the pent-up feelings of our
porters broke forth and vented themselves in peals

of laughter and shouts of triumph, together with the joyous blowing of horns, the beating of drums, and the firing off of guns.

A few days more and we arrived at Kageye, and were warmly welcomed by Gordon, who had been here for some weeks, and who, meantime, had made good progress with " Swahili," the language of Zanzibar He was being entertained by an Arab, or rather a half-bred Arab trader, named Said bin Saif; his African name is Kipanda Moto. Kageye is a wretched native village, which at that time was full of Arabs; it is a most dirty and most unhealthy place, chiefly memorable as being the spot where a young Scotch doctor, John Smith, of the Church Missionary Society, together with one of Stanley's companions, lies buried. It is near the island of Ukerewe, where Lieutenant Shergold Smith and Mr. O'Neil were murdered by the chief, Lukonge. At Kageye I spent more than six weeks, and during this time I paid a visit to Ukerewe. Gordon and Wise and myself had been strongly advised by our quondam leader Stokes, who had preceded Hannington to the coast, to fix our station on Ukerewe, and it was therefore decided that I should visit Lukonge and sound him upon the subject. Said bin Saif, the Arab mentioned before, lent me his canoe with some of his men who knew how to paddle. While it is only fair to mention this Arab's friendliness and kindness, it must not be forgotten he was paid at an exorbitant rate for

all that he did; but it was quite worth while to pay
well for the help which we received from him. We
made the journey across in one day, and found the island
of Ukerewe rich and fertile ; food, comprising dried fish,
bananas, fowls, goats, sweet potatoes, etc., is plentiful
and cheap. Unlike the tribes from Zanzibar to the
lake, the girls here are without the slightest apology
for clothing, which is one out of many indications that
ideas of propriety and modesty are perfectly arbitrary,
and vary greatly among different peoples. In Usukuma,
for instance, while the women are all most scrupulously
clothed, the men are stark naked, while in Buganda
the reverse is the case. There girls up to a marriageable
age walk about unclad without a thought of shame ;
yet the men, and even the smallest boys, are carefully
covered. It was not till the second day after my
arrival on the island that I reached Lukonge's chief
village. He received me kindly and appointed a house
for me to sleep in, and sent me some milk. The next
day I had an interview with him. I found him a very
sedate and rather handsome man. He said that he was
sorry that the first white men had been killed, and that
he would warmly welcome others who would come and
" build " * in his territory.

The death of Smith and O'Neil was a very sad affair,
and is involved in some obscurity. It seems that an
Arab trader, Sungura, had married one of Lukonge's

---

* " Build " is used in East Africa to denote settling down in a
place, ¡

daughters, and when trouble arose between the chief and the trader, the latter determined to remove his household to Kageye, and succeeded in prevailing upon the missionaries to lend him the *Daisy*, the mission-boat. He put his harem on board, and among the women was apparently the daughter of Lukonge. This action Lukonge naturally resented, as he looked upon it as an abduction, and consequently attacked the Arab, who took refuge with the missionaries, and they chivalrously defended him. Some of the natives said that while O'Neil fired on them, Smith was writing in a book all the time of the attack; they said that O'Neil succeeded in killing thirty of his assailants before he was finally overpowered. Another account says that when Smith saw he must be killed, he shot himself with his own pistol.

Mackay subsequently visited the scene of the murder, though he had great difficulty in inducing any of his followers to go with him, as they vehemently asserted that he would be killed. Lukonge, however, received him courteously, and actually restored a quantity of property which had belonged to the murdered Englishmen. During my visit I had a bad attack of fever, but I was able to present my gift to the chief. It was a piece of copper wire; and he was much pleased, and gave me in return a cow, which it was necessary to kill at once. I had therefore plenty of butcher's meat, but as I had run short of cloth, I could buy hardly sufficient food of other kinds to last us

during the return journey to the mainland. One rather
amusing incident occurred before I took my departure from the island. I was lying under a tree, lazily
watching the blue waters of the Nyanza rippling in the
sunlight while waiting for the canoe which was to take
me back to Kageye. A few yards from me a woman
was busily employed hocing a plot of ground, when presently up came an inquisitive fellow. Perhaps he was
merely of an inquiring and observant nature; but he
suddenly was attracted by the extraordinary sight of a
white man lying under a tree, clothed from head to foot
in garments such as he had never before even imagined.
He hurried across the cultivated ground in order to
make a closer inspection of such a curious phenomenon.
But the unwritten law that trespassers will be prose-
cuted was put into swift and unexpected execution by
the dusky daughter of Eve whose garden he was
desecrating. Raising her hoe, she struck the unhappy
intruder a heavy blow, which she repeated as quickly
as she was able. At first he was utterly taken by surprise; but as soon as he recovered himself, he promptly
repaid the attention with interest. After a short
scrimmage they parted in hot anger; he, objurgating and
spitting on the ground, made off to his own village,
while she hastened to her home, which lay in the
opposite direction, to gather her faction. Very soon I
saw issuing from each village, an angry and excited
crowd. I quite expected that it would end in a pitched
battle, but more peaceable counsels prevailed and the

elders on both sides sat down to hold a long palaver
and to discuss the whole question. At this juncture
my canoe arrived and I not unwillingly left them to
settle the matter by themselves. What the result was
I never heard; but no doubt the danger of broken heads
was averted when the contending parties had once
sufficiently controlled themselves to sit down for
what an African likes even better than a battle—a
long "shauri," *i.e.* discussion.

I had arranged to take a passage in Said bin Saif's
dhow, which arrived from Buganda laden with ivory
and slaves a few days after my return from Ukerewe.
She came into port hidden in a cloud of smoke from
the guns of the Arabs and their retainers on board,
who were firing a salute, which is the negroes' highest
idea of expressing satisfaction. The dhow was lying
at anchor opposite the house where I lived; but the
morning after her arrival, when I looked out on the
lake, she had disappeared. She had slipped her cable
in the night and been dashed to pieces on the rocks
which surround Kageye. The Arab bore his loss with
even more equanimity than I did. It was Allah's will,
and he would build another. However, it turned out
well for me, for in a few more weeks thirty canoes
arrived from Mutesa to bring on the new Muzungu
(white man) and two Arab traders who were bound for
Buganda. From one of these fellow-travellers I received
no little kindness. I was very ill during nearly the
whole of the twenty days' journey in the canoes, and

old Said bin Hadj used often to help with his own hand
in putting up my tent, and whenever he killed a goat
he never omitted to send me a nice joint, though I had
little except some tea to give him in return.

The canoes partly coasted along the west shores of
the lake, and partly took advantage of the islands,
making from one to another, but at sunset we always
landed, whether on the coast or on an island, to pitch
our tents and to sleep. While encamped on one of
these islands, Kyakwogera,* the officer whom Mutesa
had sent for me, took all his men off to raid a
neighbouring island. He killed the few men whom he
found there, slaughtered and cut up the cattle, and put
the meat into his boats, and brought away alive the goats
and sheep and women and children. When Kyakwogera and his men arrived, they set to work to devour the
meat, and what they could not eat they dried over fires.
It was pitiable to see how miserably ill they made
themselves by sheer over-eating. Consequently, the
next day, when we were once more on the lake, only
a few of them were able to make any attempt at
paddling the great canoe.

Among the prisoners was a little boy whom they
called Kazinja. His real name was Kangire. He
and his mother were seized and brought away together, and one of my followers purchased him with
a coat which he had stolen. When both transactions
came to light, we made him hand Kazinja over to the

* He was afterwards killed on the mainland near this very place.

mission as compensation for the theft of the coat. The child was eventually baptized, and went by the name of Bobby. He learned to read fluently and could sing hymns admirably and say prayers to perfection; but he belonged to a class which should be clearly distinguished from that of people who believe in Christ from deep personal conviction. If the existence of such a class were always recognised, it would do away with the slurs so often cast upon so-called converts. Bobby was a little liar born and bred; he could not keep his little fingers out of any tin or box or other receptacle for things pleasant to the sight and desirable for food. Though he could take the cover off a tin as well as any one, I caught him one day *flagrante delicto* owing to his inability to replace it properly, and on that occasion he got his deserts in the shape of a sound thrashing.

The poor little lad lost his mother on this voyage, and it was as well, for he was now separated from her for ever, as she would have been sold probably to one of the Arabs, and taken away never more to see her little Kangire in this world. The canoe in which she was travelling was upset by a hippopotamus, and she and two others were drowned.

We skirted the territories governed by Roma on the south up to those of Kigaju, his neighbour, and on past Kaitaba, pro-king of the Baziba; passing the important rivers the Katonga and Kagera we coasted along Budu, whose chief Pokino was one of the great Earls of

Buganda. Making our way along by the Archipelago of
the Sesse Isles, we finally landed at a place called Entebe,
about thirty miles from Mutesa's Lubiri, or capital.

A tremendous blowing off of gunpowder by my Arab
companions announced our arrival, and directly we
landed I made up the letters for Mackay and his companion, and sent two of my men off to the mission
with them. The following day Mackay himself
arrived, and gave me a warm and kindly welcome. I
looked with intense interest upon the man with whom
for the next few years I was to be so closely associated,
and of whom I had heard so much; and who had
remained at his post with such indomitable courage
and patient perseverance. General Gordon had wished
to secure him as one of his lieutenants in the Soudan;
but Mackay preferred to do his self-denying work for
Africa humbly as an English missionary rather than in
the more pompous guise of an Egyptian pasha.*

As soon as Mackay met me my travelling troubles
were at an end. He had brought a fine Muscat donkey
down to the port to meet me. I gladly mounted and
preceded him to the mission station, where I was kindly
received by his fellow-missionary, Rev. P. O'Flaherty,
who showed me my new quarters in the comfortable
house which Mackay had built. How I first became
acquainted with King Mutesa I must leave for another
chapter.

---

* Mr. Mackay has been lately decorated by the Khedive with the
order of the Osmanieh of the 4th class for his services to Emin Pasha.

CHAPTER VI.

I now come to the important figure of one of the two kings after whom I have named this book: Mutesa,* Kabaka † of Buganda, overlord of Buynoro, Busoga, Buzongora, Karagwe, Buzinja, and other peoples, nations, and languages—son of Suna, grandson of Kamanya, descendant of the Divine Kintu, who traces his descent for so many generations back as to put to shame the pedigrees of most of the inhabitants of these isles who boast the possession of a pedigree at all.

That he was of Bahuma descent there can be little doubt—the despised Bahuma,‡ or Wahuma, are the herdsmen in Buganda.

Mutesa succeeded to the kingdom on the death of Suna, a cruel, cold-blooded, and ferocious tyrant, who died miserably of small-pox while conducting one of the bloody raids for which the Baganda are infamously

---

* Mutesa, not Mtesa, which the Baganda could not say any more than the ordinary Englishman, who generally calls the name "teaser."

† Kabaka means "kaiser."

‡ The Bahuma or Wahuma in Buganda are called Bayima; the Baganda have no "h." Is it not curious that we change the Greek "u" into a "y" sound?

famous. He was feared and hated by his people, and it
is said that those who were deputed to bear the corpse
of the deceased Kabaka back to the capital for burial,
dashed it down to the ground with scornful fury, as if to
wreak an impotent vengeance upon the dead. The quiet-
looking, large-eyed lad Mutesa was chosen to succeed
his warrior father. He, however, soon earned and took
the significant name of " Causer of tears," "Mukaa-
bya," and by this name he was usually known; but he
was still oftener styled simply "Kabaka," or the King.
Before officially "eating Buganda," as it is called, he
had to go and seat himself on the stone throne which
has been used for the purpose from time immemorial,
and which is some distance from Rubaga, where he
afterwards made his capital. When I knew him, only
one of his numerous brothers was left, the others
having, on various excuses, been put to death. The
survivor was a very meek-looking, insignificant man,
with a face scarred with small-pox, yet with a distinct
resemblance to the king; possibly his inoffensiveness
and insignificance accounts for the fact of his
lengthened existence.

Mutesa soon sent down to the mission-house to say
that he wished to see the newly-arrived "Muzungu,"
"white man," and it was accordingly decided that though
I was far from well, I had better accede to his majesty's
commands. I therefore arrayed myself in my longest
black coat, in order to pay fitting respect to the great
monarch to whom I was about to have the high honour

of being introduced. And so I mounted upon the fine
Muscat donkey aforesaid, which the king had presented to the missionaries, and, convoyed by Mr.
O'Flaherty, I started for the palace. Turning off the
magnificent sweep of road which led up to Rubaga, the
now deserted capital, we passed along a beautiful lane,
between lofty fences, "bisakati," formed of the tall
tiger-grass which grows so abundantly in Buganda,
and is used in making the enclosures which surround
the houses and gardens of the upper classes. These
fences are made by driving posts of some ten or twelve
feet high into the ground at intervals of a few yards,
to which are fastened horizontally long thick ropes of
the reed-like grass-stalks. These form rails, of which
there may be from four to nine, according to the height
of the fence. To the rails are tied vertically stalks
of the same grass in couples, thus making a smooth,
close-fitting palisade. These fences look very neat,
but constantly require to be repaired. Their erection
is a regular craft, and forms part of the training of the
youth of Buganda, and every feudal lord has the right
to call upon his vassals for this service.

The way wound between groves of carefully cultivated bananas, "bitoki," where we saw women (who
do all the gardening) carefully lop off the withered
branches, and spread them along the ground to prevent
the growth of weeds or grass.

We also passed by sweet potatoes planted in ridges,
which were being weeded by some women, who, in the

E

interval of labour, were enjoying a quiet smoke. This curious habit, so common among men in Europe, prevails also all over East Africa, and is largely indulged in by women. The Wanyamwezi men, however, prefer snuff, leaving smoke to the female sex. The people of Ukerewe, Lukonge's island, mix powdered tobacco with water and then " snuffle " it up their noses.

We now came out on another magnificently wide road, which led in a straight line to Nabulagala, Mutesa's present palace—a road even wider than the widest street of the Irish capital. Presently we ascended a slight incline in front of us, from the top of which we obtained a splendid view of the surrounding country. Hills rose up on all sides, covered to their very summits with the rich and vivid green of banana groves. Away to the north-west were the purple hills of distant Bulemezi, one of the provinces, or earldoms, of Buganda. Behind us was the saddle-backed hill Mutundwe, with its solitary tree, a landmark for miles round ; while before us, on its perfectly bare eminence, lay Nabulagala, the "lubire," or head-quarters, of Mutesa—a vast village of gigantic straw-built houses.

As my guide was pointing out to me the beauty of the view, a little page came panting up, his snowy cotton robe flowing behind him, to bid us make more haste. He wore the "luga," or necklet of bent cane, to show that he was one of the Kabaka's "baddu," slaves, or rather " bagalagala," pages. He made no salutation, but simply uttered the word "Jangu," "Come."

Soon another little fellow came running up, and he
in his turn uttered the word "Yanguyako," "Be
quick." These little pages have all the insolence of
office, derived from the brief authority with which they
are invested. Their names were probably Mukassa and
Musoke, which in Buganda are as common as Duncan
and Donald in the Highlands.

A succession of messengers met us until we reached
the "Wankaki," or royal gateway. All the gateways
which lead to "majesty" have names, and are kept by
officers called "Bagazi," *i.e.* hall porters. If Swift had
only been possessed of missionary proclivities, the
world might have had a voyage to Buganda instead of
a voyage to Lilliput. The heart would grow sick with
scorn of all this beggarly pomp and paltry pride, were
it not that here, as in Europe, in spite of it all, and
across it all, there are found sterling qualities, generous impulses, and noble aspirations.

When the wide "Wankaki" was passed, we found ourselves in a spacious court, in which were one or two
houses, the largest being the official residence of the
king's head wife, or "Kadu lubarè." The houses of all the
chiefs and upper classes in the country are exact models
of the king's, only of course upon a much smaller scale.

The palisade which surrounds the "Kibuga," or
royal enclosure, is different from the fence of all other
persons in the country, with the exception of the
priests of Lubarê and the king's eldest son. I have
not seen the enclosures of the two queens in Buganda,

E 2

"Namasolè," mother of the king, and "Lubuga," sister
of the king; but possibly they may possess the privilege
of making their fences in the same style as the king.
The difference between these sacred and royal palisades
and the ordinary enclosure consists in the fact that
the former are made with the reeds or tiger-grass
crossed and wattled, while in the latter they are simply
placed side by side.

Strange it seemed to find oneself, for the first time,
in one of the great capitals of Africa. It was a bright
and busy scene, and we were soon surrounded by a
curious and noisy crowd. Here were people of all
shades and complexions, from a light copper colour to
jetty black. In front of us, going in the direction of the
next gateway, towered the gigantic figure (nearly seven
feet high) of Katorogo, the king's head "Muhuma,"
herdsman, though Sebalija is the Muganda chief
who is responsible for the Kabaka's cattle. Katorogo was followed by a skin-clad company, whose dress
presented a striking contrast to the brighter and
more showy garments of the other courtiers. Among
the ever-moving throng were musicians from Busoga,
with their mud-coloured back-cloths easily distin-
guishable from the light brown or red cloths of the
Baganda. Again, the "Bajona," or potters, are passing
along, bearing on their heads enormous earthenware
vessels, which they are about to present as tribute to
the Kabaka. Behind us a great chief has just entered,
clothed in a scarlet coat of fine English cloth richly

embroidered with gold, all native work, and with bright pink trousers of the same material. This is Mukwenda, Earl of Singo; he is followed by a motley crowd of vassals—a wee slave boy bearing his pipe and shoes, other slaves carrying his gracefully decanter-shaped bottle gourd with its exquisitely worked "luseke," a long bent tube, on the outside of which is plaited beautiful fine-coloured grass. Mukwenda stalks along with the air of an emperor. But his peers do not forget that though he is an earl to-day, he is a mere mushroom nobleman, a parvenu, a peasant. Only a few years ago he was but a miserable "mugoma" or drummer—a harlequin on whom the royal favour had lighted. He carries in his hand a long curiously-shaped white staff, which has been polished with Nature's own glass-paper, the rough leaves of a certain tree which are called "luwawo." On his head he wears a red fez. He, like us, has come to "kika," that is to present himself at Mutesa's grand "lukiko," or levee. All this time I was mounted on the donkey, and we pushed our way onward through the throng of hurrying courtiers, till we approached a second gateway. Through this I caught a glimpse of the scarlet coats of several stately chiefs. But just as we were about to enter, a sliding gate of reeds was rudely drawn across our path, and immediately fastened with the thin leather thong used for the purpose. My companion, Mr. O'Flaherty, however, was quite equal to the occasion, and whipping out his pocket-knife he cut the thong and forced open the door, then seizing the bridle of the donkey in one hand and waving his stick in the other, he led me triumphantly through, the guards fleeing right and left upon our approach. We soon squeezed through another gateway. Here I dismounted, and we now entered the third court, and made straight for one of the largest houses which it contained—the usual straw-built, pole-supported, beehive-shaped hut of the country. Within this, on a mat, was sitting a splendid-looking man with a very handsome face; all about him were seated chiefs, like himself, blazing in crimson and gold, and so thought I this must be the far-famed Mutesa. He motioned me to be seated near him, and then entered into conversation with my companion. The space behind the chieftain was occupied by a miscellaneous assemblage of peasants, retainers, litigants, slaves, and minstrels. The supposed king was evidently of the Bahuma tribe, or else, like so many of the Baganda, had much Bahuma blood in his veins. When we had sat here for some time, Mr. O'Flaherty got up, saying, "Let us go now and see the 'Katikiro,' 'chief judge.'" On getting outside I asked him who the handsome chief might be. "That," he replied, "is Kyambalango, the 'Kymbugwe' or keeper of the palace."

Passing through yet another gateway we came to the chief judge's court-house or " Kigango." The chief judge or chancellor, like the chief whom we had just left, was seated on a mat and surrounded by a still greater crowd. On our approach he rose and came out to meet us, and

received us very graciously; he was dressed in Arab
costume, a snowy white gown of fine cotton, over
which he wore a long mantle or robe of rich black cloth,
heavily embroidered with gold. He was small, very
handsome, evidently of Bahuma blood, though darker
than the Bahuma usually are. This is the man of
whom Stanley has given so admirable a description—
suave, polite, shrewd, far-seeing; but also cold, cruel,
cunning, false and treacherous. The Bismarck of
Buganda and virtual ruler of the kingdom—this was
the man of boundless ambition and intolerable pride
whose self-will and masterdom would not endure to
be thwarted, and woe to any one who crossed his
path! This was the man who in stormy passion had
flung down his cap in presence of the king, and had
refused to relinquish his suit until Mutesa had stripped
a powerful rival chief of everything to gratify the spite
of his imperious chancellor.

The Katikiro made room for me on his own mat—a
high honour which I am afraid at that time I took as
a matter of course.

I watched the great man as he listened to the counsel
who were arguing the cases on which he was to give
judgment, "sala musango," "cut judgment," he all the
while playing the game of "Mweso."* He was never-

* The game of "Mweso," or "Bao," is played on a board, in which
are cut thirty-two square holes; hard nuts, beans, or bullets are
used as counters. It is common all over East Africa. The object
of the game is to secure your adversaries' counters. It requires
quickness in counting.

theless listening carefully, though you would hardly think so to see his lithe fingers gathering up the counters with which he played and dropping them into their proper holes. He would suddenly stop, arrange some small white sticks in order on the ground to mark the points of his summing up, and then give judgment, though the scale could be made to incline this way or that by a timely bribe. On hearing the verdict, both plaintiff and defendant and their supporters energetically thanked the judge. Kneeling before him and clasping their hands, they moved them up and down, crying out, "Neyanze, Neyanze, Neyanzege," or, speaking in the plural, "Tweyanze, Tweanzege," "We thank you."

Suddenly there pealed out a long rolling tattoo from the deep-toned royal drums, accompanied by a loud blare of trumpets, which had been a present from England to Mutesa. The music was what might be expected from the tuning up of such instruments preliminary to the production of some melody or air; but possibly the musicians may have been playing a composition of Wagner's which my ear was not well enough trained to recognise. At any rate this was my first summons to the great "Lukiko" or "levee "of the king.

Immediately the chief judge arose, and in another minute his Kigango was deserted, as he, accompanied by the other earls, entered the precincts of the great court of the Kabaka. The chief judge, besides being Katikiro of Buganda, held also the Earldom of Kyagwe. We followed in the rear of the earls, jostled with scarlet-coated Buganda nobles and tributary kings.

Among the throng hastening to pay their respects to the majesty of Buganda were representatives of the Bahuma lords or Bakama, as well as chiefs from Busoga. The fair-faced Lubambula of Koki from the west, and the scowling Wakoli, paramount chief of Busoga, who divided with Luba—known as being the captor of Bishop Hannington—authority to the east of Buganda. Here too were obsequious smiling Arabs from Muscat—men who can smile and smile and be villains with it all; pale-faced Englishmen from the cold North; runaway Egyptian soldiers from the Soudan; adventurers from the east coast and Madagascar; mountebanks, minstrels, dancers, dwarfs. This rabble found seats in the best places they could command outside, while we followed the earls through Mutesa's body-guard, which were drawn up in line, forming a passage reaching up to the entrance to the king's palace.

CHAPTER VII.

KING MUTESA's great reception-house was a vast beehive-like building, supported on lofty wooden posts which ran in four not very regular rows. I was disappointed at my first view of the Kabaka's straw-built palace. Here there was no attempt at ornament of any kind such as I had seen at Mirambo's Gwikuru, no Arab wood-carving, and no stone or plaster work. The workmanship of Buganda was, however, represented in its highest excellence—fine grass and string and reed work, exquisite indeed, and perfect of its kind, but nothing enduring.

I could not help thinking that this hill on which was built the city of the king, in a few more years would be as desolate and deserted as Rubaga now was. The whole nation might pass away without leaving a trace of its existence, except perhaps in a few metal ornaments and weapons, which might come to light in some future age.

But enough of my reveries. We entered the wide doorway of the house where Mutesa was. The king lay reclining upon a low couch, beneath a shabby canopy of dirty bark-cloth. The couch was placed at the right-

hand side of the entrance. The king was clothed from
head to foot in a snowy white robe, and lay back holding
in his right hand a small round looking-glass, in which
he could see reflected the faces of the courtiers who
clustered round the doorway without. At the foot of
the couch were two handsome boys, their bodies shining
with a superabundance of oil. They too were dressed
in snowy cotton robes. One was clasping his royal
master's feet, and warming them with his hands, while
the other held himself in readiness to brush away any
miserable fly whose brain was too undeveloped to
comprehend the awful majesty of its fellow-mortal,
upon whom it sacrilegiously dared to settle. It is the
custom that every great chief shall give some of his
sons to the king to be his pages or "bagalagala,"
and it is from these that future lords and nobles are
recruited. Little Nyonyi Entono ("the small bird"),
not allowed yet to enter the presence of the king, but
a sub-page in one of the great houses outside, in no
long time will reach man's estate, and find himself
standing in the mighty Katikiro's shoes. And little
Kagwa, quickly grown to manhood, by the strange turn
of fortune's wheel will find himself a mighty earl—
Mukwenda, Lord of Singo; but before they reach that
uncertain eminence, they will have to suffer much
both of torture and of shame.

At the head of the couch, kneeling half outside, and
with his head inclined so as to be near the king's ear,
was Kolugi, chief storekeeper. He, though not noble,

and therefore not allowed inside the presence-chamber, was a man of great influence and power, and was always more or less our staunch friend.

Inside, and sitting on a mat near the king's head, was his favourite chief Kyambalango (" Leopard-clothed ") or " Kyimbugwe ; " whilst facing Kyambalango, sat the imperious chancellor. On the left of the doorway, on entering, were seated also on the ground two or three rows of the great lords, while in the space between the chiefs and the king camp-stools were placed for Mr. O'Flaherty and myself.

Further away, in the interior of the house, and facing the entrance, were seated a bevy of black beauties— the ladies or Bakyala of the king's household.

Strange to say, that while Europeans and Arabs immediately single out the light copper-coloured, beautiful hazel-eyed Bahuma women as bearing the palm of beauty, Mutesa and his chiefs admired rather the stouter-built women of a more decidedly pronounced negro type.

When we came into the royal presence, I was duly introduced to the king. I took off my hat, and made him a bow, which he acknowledged Arab fashion with an inclination of his head and by placing his hand upon his heart. He then motioned me to be seated on the camp-stool, a high honour rarely conferred even upon native chiefs, but generally granted to European visitors, though the Arabs were always made to sit on the floor.

I was the bearer of a handsome present of some fine
scarlet cloth, which the Church Missionary Society had
sent to the king. This Mr. O'Flaherty presented, at
the same time dilating upon my virtues, dignity and
importance; though I of course was quite ignorant of
what was passing.

After a little, a skilled male dancer appeared, and went
through the surprising evolutions and contortions of
the strange body dance, which I had seen the women
of Unyamwesi performing. However, whether it was
watching the mazy motion of the dance, or whether it
was my own weariness coupled with the heat of the
reception-hall, I became intolerably drowsy, and was
only awakened to the realities of my position by being
addressed directly by the sovereign. I felt like a
person at church suddenly conscious of having been
caught napping, and tried to look as if I were quite
wide awake. I did not of course know what Mutesa
said, but my companion explained that he was
commanding me to turn round that he might get a
better view of me. This I did. "Now to the other
side." I did so. And then his majesty pronounced the
pleasing verdict that I was " Mulungi," a word which
means good or beautiful, to which all the chiefs
assented cordially, as they would have done had the
monarch been pleased to say the reverse.

I have no doubt that important business of the
kingdom was transacted at this Lukiko, but the language
was utterly unintelligible to me, so that I was not sorry

when we were all suddenly dismissed by a quick motion of the king's hand. Out we streamed as we had come in ; and thus came to an end the great duty of the day, and every one was now free to follow his own devices until the next "baraza," levee, of the Kabaka was announced.

A few days after this, I went again with Mr. O'Flaherty to see the king, and on this occasion we had a private interview. A great number of the king's wives and other members of his harem were present. His Majesty was most affable and agreeable, and again repeated his verdict of the former occasion, that I was "Mulungi," and even said that I was worthy of one of his own daughters. He had thoughtfully, a day or two before, sent down to offer me a wife. I was ill at the time, and so Mackay kindly or unkindly, according to the view taken, refused her for me.

When Mutesa remarked that I ought to have a Mumbeja or princess, there was a shrill chorus from the ladies of "Wewawo,"—"Yes, indeed."

Mr. O'Flaherty remarked, in making polite excuses for me, that white people like to marry white people, as black people like to marry those of the same colour as themselves. Again the shrill chorus of female voices— "Oh no, but we like white men very much." After a little more badinage the interview was concluded. Mutesa never in the presence of any women indulged his perverted taste for vile conversation, which at any rate was one of many indications that there existed in

Buganda a respect for women, and also showed that the king felt and knew that such conversation was really shameful and wrong.

I used generally to visit Mutesa once a month, and to his amusement, one day, I read him a fable which I had been told by one of the people, and which I had printed in a small press which we had. I used also to take up a translation of a few verses of the Bible, and he always most courteously allowed me to read it to him. The Arabs used to bring the Koran, and intone passages which neither they nor the king understood ; still Mutesa's verdict was that the Arabs' rendering of the Koran was vastly superior to my poor translations into his own language. I have no doubt that if I had intoned the Litany in English for his edification, I should have run the Arabs very close in the competition.

I remember being present once at the king's levee when news arrived of a severe defeat which the Baganda had suffered on one of their raids, at the hands of a people called Bakede, to the north-east of Buganda. The news was received by the king and his nobles with the utmost composure. Mutesa could lose an army with as much outward equanimity, at any rate, as a chess-player would lose a pawn.

On this occasion the Baganda had raided the naked Bakede, they had taken them at a disadvantage, and had collected vast numbers of cattle and little children. The Bakede women would not accompany the successful warriors, and preferred death, be it said to their honour, to the shame that awaited them—a fate which was speedily meted out to them.

The first party got safely across the frontier; but the Bakede meanwhile had gathered in force, and intercepted the second division; and the Baganda, in spite of their guns, were utterly annihilated by the spears of their warlike assailants.

I may here give an account of my last interview with Mutesa. We had heard that there was to be a grand "Kiwendo," or human sacrifice, at the next feast of the Lubare, or Demiurge of Buganda, who, unlike the sublime "Katonda" ("Creator"), interests himself in the affairs of men, and to whom sacrifices and offerings are constantly made. We thought it our duty to remonstrate with the king, and to attempt to dissuade him from so great a crime. We accordingly wrote him a letter, which I was deputed to deliver. As a rule Mutesa liked receiving letters, though this time he utterly refused it. We had sent a letter to him on a former occasion to ask him not to take revenge on the Bakede for having annihilated his army; no revenge expedition as a matter of fact was sent, but whether from fear of God or fear of the Bakede I should not like to hazard an opinion.

As I made my way to the king's enclosure, a little incident occurred which aptly illustrates one of the customs of the country. When I turned into the main road leading to Nabulagala, I overtook a large party of women, the harem of some great chief, preceded by a small boy. In Buganda, small boys are the custodians of the women. The Arabs had tried to prevail upon Mutesa to copy their own customs with reference to the custody of his harem ; and though the king followed their evil counsel in the case of a few of his pages, the general custom still was that young boys should hold the office of the keeping of the women.

The little boy in question carried a large thick stick, not altogether for ornament, and marched at the head of his convoy. A poor peasant was coming in the opposite direction, carrying some sweet potatoes on his head, doubtless his day's food. At a signal from the Kadu Lubare (head wife), the youngster in charge swaggered up to him and ordered him to stand and deliver. The man, not liking to lose his dinner, demurred, whereupon the urchin began to lay his heavy stick across the back of this insolent slave who dared to refuse his potatoes to his superiors. I had stopped my donkey, and was watching the scene with much interest and amusement, but when the peasant began to receive a cudgelling, I thought it past a joke, so I slipped down and came up suddenly behind the young brave and put my arms round him. He at once became powerless, and the owner of the potatoes made off as quickly as he could. The ladies and their young squire began to abuse me roundly for having so rudely interfered. I replied by grabbing the boy's fine stick, and then remounted the donkey and went on. He came and begged hard for it : " Munange sebo mpa

mugo gwange " ("My friend, sir, give me my stick").
But I said, "No, I was good before I saw you, but
you have taught me to steal, and I like your stick."
He had to content himself with my reply, and I
left him to digest this practical sermon on the eighth
commandment. I had seen a similar party a few days
previously meet a little girl, and quietly strip her of her
clothing, and leave her to go her way without a single
rag. It is the custom that the great and powerful have
carte blanche to seize people on the road, and take
whatever they are carrying. Sometimes women, hoeing
near the road-side, will capture a passer-by, and, on
pain of a severe castigation or of robbing him, will
make him take a turn at the spade while they have
a smoke.

This custom leads to endless litigation, for if B.'s
wives rob A.'s slaves, and A. happens to be a bigger
man than B., there is material for a very pretty quarrel
and lawsuit.

Soon after arriving at the great enclosure, the king's
baraza was announced, and the crowd of chiefs,
courtiers, peasants, foreigners, dancers, musicians, and
others surged through the doors into the royal court of
reception. On this occasion the Kabaka was keeping
great state, and was sitting, dressed in native costume,
upon a rude chair, over which a leopard skin had been
thrown. A costly dark-red scented lubugu, or bark-
cloth robe, was knotted over his right shoulder; he wore
a collar or thick necklet of finest bead-work round his

neck, and he sat with a long scimitar between his knees. Possibly he was sitting up, to make people believe that he was recovering from his illness, and to give Kabarega the idea that he was strong and able. Kabarega is the present King of Bunyoro (described by Sir Samuel Baker), with whom the Baganda wage incessant warfare. Kyambalango, the favourite, sat at the king's feet, while the other great earls sat opposite. We were not in the usual reception-hall, but in a smaller and less roomy building.

When the crush was over, I walked in and made my bow to Mutesa, but was rudely bidden by some of the earls to go and sit outside with the inferior chiefs and with the Arab teacher, or Mwalimu, as he called himself, who had lately arrived, and been very favourably received by the king. Such an indignity had not been offered to any European before, though on another occasion, when Mackay and I attended a grand lukiko, the insolent chancellor had made us sit far behind, and had refused us chairs, saying, " Do not I sit on the ground, and who are you ? " On that occasion, Mackay got up and appealed to the king, and made such an impression that he gave an order, and, amid the acclamations of the servile earls, chairs were brought, and we were allowed to sit quite close to the king himself. The chancellor gave us his hand, and congratulated us with a smiling face, saying, " Muli baganze lero " (" You are favourites to-day "). Knowing that the kindly Kabaka would probably be inclined to

F 2

treat me politely, and that this was only an officious order prompted by the jealousy of the chiefs, I simply turned to Mutesa and said, "Sikiriza okutula ebweru" ("I do not agree to sit outside"), and then turned away to walk off in a huff. I was called back immediately, and the king said to me, "Where do you want to sit?" "Here, in your presence," I replied; and the gracious monarch immediately motioned to me to sit down beside Earl Mukwenda.

The proceedings began by a display of native dancing, as already described, accompanied by a Musoga minstrel on the "Nanga," a kind of banjo. When there was a lull in the music, I thought that it would be a good opportunity to present my letter, which I produced, and the king's eye fell upon it. I said, "I have brought a letter;" but the king pretended not to hear, and looked away from me, so that he might not see my outstretched hand.

At this juncture, the king's Koran was brought and handed to the little Arab mwalimu; but before reading he turned the book over, and pointed out something to the king. Mutesa's countenance, usually so benign, suddenly changed to scowling anger, and with flashing eyes he caught the book from the Arab, and shook it in his outstretched hand towards me, saying at the same time, "You have spoilt my book. Do you wish to insult me?" As may be imagined, I was perfectly astonished at this unlooked-for outburst of anger, nor did it dawn upon me at first what connection there

could be between the king's Koran and myself. I
suddenly remembered, however, that the king had sent
the book down to the Mission to be mended, and
Mackay had turned the covers the wrong way about
to facilitate the operation. The Arab had pointed
this out to the king, and sat with a meekly satisfied
air, enjoying my discomfiture, although he was a
particular friend of mine, and used to visit me
constantly.

I took out a new linen pocket-handkerchief, and told
Kyambalango that this was for the king. The chief
received it, but said that the king was angry, and
would not accept my peace-offering. It did not,
however, occur to Kyambalango to return it. Pocket-
handkerchiefs are quite an institution in Buganda,
but it is not etiquette to use one in public. So,
unless you wish to be thought an ignorant boor or
foreigner, you retire for a minute or two to blow your
nose, the handkerchief being a small square of bark-
cloth. I have seen a chief make use of the garment of
one of his attendants. Colds are very common, and
as it is considered impolite to speak of certain ailments,
they are euphemistically described as " colds," (" sen-
yiga ") in which condition a large majority of the adult
population constantly remain.

But to return. The king refused both my letter and
my pocket-handkerchief, and I was not sorry to see
him raise his hand and wave a signal that the reception
had come to an end. Rather sadly I left; and this was

the last time I ever saw the king. As I mounted the donkey to return home, the little laddie whose stick I had stolen was waiting to beg for it back again, and I was very happy to return it to him, so we parted mutually satisfied. Mutesa did not live very long after this reception and died in the autumn of 1884.

CHAPTER VIII.

MUTESA'S DEATH.

MUTESA had long been ailing, and seemed to grow daily worse and worse; the Arabs, however, assured him that there were some traders from Zanzibar, now at Unyamyembe, in the Unyamwezi country, who possessed a marvellous medicine which could cure him. Messengers were accordingly despatched post haste to bring these great doctors with their potent prescriptions, and they arrived in due time, and at once commenced operations. It was given out that the medicine was "dungi enyo" (very good), but that no one would be allowed to see the king whilst the drug was working. Mutesa was ordered a particular diet, and forbidden to eat salt (black people as a rule never eat salt when they are ill, why I do not know). It was reported that Mutesa endured the treatment for some time, but, as the new regimen prevented him from enjoying the society of his wives, he grew tired of his doctors, and refused any longer to follow their advice.

The condition of the king was kept a profound secret, and even when he died the event was not made known till some time after it had taken place. Whether, as was reported, the Arabs' medicine had proved fatal rather than curative, or whether he was smothered by some of his wives, will never be known. The latter alternative is by no means impossible, for, as Emin Pasha shows, the practice is not confined to Buganda.

The possibility that the king's death might prove a very serious matter for us had of course been in our minds, though we did not suspect that the end was so near. From the inquiries which we made of the converts, and from the accounts of previous visitors to Buganda, we were led to expect that there would be a wild scene of anarchy and confusion upon the death of Mutesa, and probably a bloody civil war. However, as the sequel will show, these apprehensions were not fulfilled, and the interregnum passed in comparative calm.

One night, as Mr. O'Flaherty was sitting up late writing home letters, at about half-past twelve, he heard a low voice outside his window, and on going out he found one of the native Christians who had come down with a friend to warn us that the king was dead. I slept in a room up-stairs, and he came up immediately and aroused me. When I opened the door, he seemed much agitated, and said, "Mukassa of the drum has just come down to tell us that the king is dead." He added in a dubious tone that he did not suppose that they would kill us. We could now hear the quick beat of drums, sudden and alarming, and the sound of a great cry swept fitfully and wildly across the intervening valleys, as ever and anon a gust of wind stronger than

usual brought it to our ears. We got out all our
available guns, fearing that the rabble, now let loose,
might make a sudden attack upon the mission ; and I
loaded my revolver, putting it at my head, and then lay
down to restless sleep and troubled dreams.

In the morning, Tom the coffee-maker before mentioned, was early stirring, and when I looked out of
my window, he saw me, and put his hand to his mouth,
and said in a stage whisper, "Sultani amekufa" (the
sultan is dead). Soon afterwards I awakened my little
boy Lugalama, who slept upstairs near me, and told him
that the king was dead ; he said with great consternation, " Munange tunakola tutiya ? " My friend, what
shall we do ? It was indeed an alarming piece of news
for us all. It might mean the total destruction of the
mission property, and possibly the loss of our own lives
and the slavery or death of our boys.

When the great earls met in council, it was debated
whether the strangers should be attacked—namely the
Arabs and ourselves. Kyambalango, our supposed
friend, and Mukwenda of Singo, were in favour of robbing
us ; but the clear-headed Katikiro (chief judge) combated
their proposal on the ground that it would discourage
the visits of strangers and the development of trade.

The Arabs were all expecting an attack, and had spent
the night armed to the teeth. They had also armed
their slaves and given them gunpowder. The next
day, two men arrived from Mackay, who was down at
the lake about twelve miles off overhauling the mission

boat. On the way they had been robbed of their
clothing and had had to run for their lives. When
Mackay heard the news, he launched the boat at once,
and made her ready for sea, in case the mission should
be destroyed and we should be compelled to seek
refuge on the lake. The people who brought him news
of the king's death assured him that his place would be
plundered.

At this time every one in the country was standing
on the defensive, awaiting the onset of his neighbours,
so that there really remained nobody to make an
attack.

Meanwhile, we at the mission had gone to see the
chiefs, and to express our condolence upon the death of
Mutesa. Mr. O'Flaherty went in the morning, and I
in the afternoon, taking a present of fine calico to offer
for the king's obsequies.

As I drew near the court, I heard the sound of bitter
wailing, and on my arrival found myself among a
weeping crowd.

The principal chiefs were collected together in a little
temporary hut, sitting on the floor dressed in dirty bark-
cloths, and shedding tears piteously, while, in the great
house where the dead king lay, his wives were crying
and loudly lamenting him.

I had been told it was the custom to kill the
unsuccessful candidate for the throne, and as I was
personally interested in Mwanga and another lad, sons
of the late emperor, whom I knew, I begged the

chiefs to let that custom be omitted on the present occasion.

Great credit is due to the chancellor for his firmness and for the good order which he kept throughout the country, owing to which very few lives were lost and very little property destroyed.

The next day the chiefs sent for Mackay, with the request that he would make a coffin for Mutesa. He had already won extraordinary fame by the coffin which he had previously made for the late king's mother, Namasole. He has described the circumstance; and what follows is almost entirely in his own words.

The morning after the death of Mutesa's mother, Mackay and Mr. O'Flaherty had gone to pay their respects to the king. They found all the chiefs with their hands clasped above their heads, roaring and shedding tears with all their might. When they entered, the king bade these chiefs be silent, which they were instantaneously. His majesty then asked Mackay how royalty was buried in England. Mackay endeavoured to describe three royal coffins with cloth coverings, and one of them of lead to preserve the remains. At once the king asked him if he would be undertaker and make the coffins; and, thinking that they would be of ordinary dimensions, Mackay agreed to do so, at which Mutesa was much pleased. Mutesa, however, had no lead, but plenty of copper, which Mackay told him would do well enough.

The court was dismissed, and soon after there arrived at the mission a host of fine bronze trays of Egyptian workmanship (probably presents from General Gordon), and copper pots and water jars of Zanzibar (Hindu) make, with copper drums made in Buganda by coast artisans. These were to be manufactured into a coffin.

Next morning, he went off to Rusaka, the residence of the late queen-mother, some five miles distant, to measure the body. Much objection was made by the royal ladies there, at his going in to measure the corpse, but his friend, the chief Kyimbugwe, was the master of the ceremonies, and he explained that Mackay had been commissioned by the king to do so. Mackay was, however, somewhat taken aback, when he was told by some of the other chiefs that he ought not to have measured the corpse, but the dimensions of the grave, and have made the coffins to fit the latter. He told them that there was not copper enough in the land to make a box larger than what was necessary for the body alone, but that, if there were, he would willingly make one as large as a mountain, but that, as it was, he would make the inner coffins to suit the body, and the outer one as large as a house if they liked.

The grave was a huge pit, some twenty feet by fifteen feet at the mouth, and about thirty feet deep. It was dug in the centre of the late Queen's chief house, an enormous hut some hundred and fifty feet in diameter, as usual all roof, with no walls, and a perfect forest of poles inside, the centre ones being large enough for frigate masts. Rusaka stands on a hill of dry sandstone, clay, and gravel. It was well that the stratum was so firm, otherwise serious accidents might have happened if the sides of the grave had fallen in.

Nearly all the excavated gravel had been carried away, while the monster pit was neatly lined all round with bark-cloth. Into this several new bark-cloths were thrown, and carefully spread at the bottom, filling up much of the hole. Then the segments of the huge box, which, with the other coffins, had taken more than a month to make, were lowered in with much trouble, and Mackay descended and nailed the corners together. After this, he was summoned to the ceremony of putting the corpse into the first coffin. Thousands of women were yelling with all their might, a few with tears in their eyes. Only the ladies of the royal family were near the body, which by this time had been reduced to a mummy, by constantly squeezing out the fluids with rags of bark-cloth. It was wrapped in a new "lubugu," bark-cloth, and laid on the ground. The chiefs half filled the nicely padded coffin with " bufta," finest Manchester shirting, then several bunches of petty charms belonging to the Queen were laid in, and the body was placed in the coffin, which was immediately filled up with more calico. Kyimbugwe, Kawuta, and the other chiefs in charge, carried the coffin to the court where the grave-house was, when much more yelling took place. Mackay then screwed the lid down, but such was the attachment of some of the royal ladies to the deceased, that he had to have them peremptorily

ordered away, with their crying and tears, and hugging
of the coffin, before he could get near to perform his
duties as undertaker. Then came the copper coffin,
into which the other was lowered by means of a huge
sheet, and the lid of which had to be riveted down, a
process that was new to the chiefs standing by. " He
cuts iron like thread," they said, as the pincers snapped
the nails. " Mackay is a proper smith," they all
shouted.

With no mechanical contrivances, it was astonishing
how they got this copper coffin, with its ponderous
contents, lowered into the deep grave, without letting
it fall end foremost into the great box below. The task
was effected, however, by means of the great multitude
of men. Thousands of yards of unbleached calico
shirtings were then filled in, round and over the copper
coffin, until the big box was half full. The remainder
was filled up with bark-cloths, as also the space round
the outside of the box. The lid was lowered, and
Mackay descended once more to nail it down. Several
thousands more of "Embugu," bark-cloths, were then
laid on, until within three feet of the surface, when
earth was thrown in, to the level of the floor of the
house where the grave was.

Mackay and his companion returned at dusk, but the
burying was not completed till nearly midnight. Next
morning, every man, woman, and child in the land had
their heads shaved, and put off their mourning dress of
tattered bark-cloth, "luzina," and belt of plantain leaf.

The amount of property in calico and bark-cloth, buried with Namasole, was estimated at fifteen thousand pounds. Mackay ends this most interesting description by saying, " Who would have thought in the civilised world of burying fifteen thousand pounds worth of cloth in the grave of even a queen ? "

But to return to the subject of Mutesa's own obsequies. At first the native smiths and carpenters undertook to make the coffins by their own unaided efforts, but the attempt was such a miserable failure that the chiefs had to beg Mackay to show them how the work was to be done. They said that there must be three coffins at least; but Mackay begged them to allow two to suffice. He then made a huge chest, on which he nailed brass and copper trays flattened out, and copper sheathing, together with the zinc lining of old cases which we had received filled with various stores. The copper and zinc represented the metal coffin, and the whole was covered on the outside with the fine white calico which in Buganda is only worn by the upper classes. The effect was considered satisfactory, and so the dead king was placed in this novel coffin, and buried in a grave which was dug in one of his largest houses.

The whole country went into mourning, and every one allowed his hair to grow.* No white or coloured cloths were seen; the men were all clothed in the national costume of ·bark-cloth, knotted over the right

* In mourning, the ancient Egyptians allowed the hair and beard to grow. Herodotus, II. 36.

shoulder, but girded as a sign of mourning, with withered plantain fibre, an emblem of decay and death. The women also wore the bark-cloth wrapped round them, under their arms so as to cover the bosom. A casual observer would not notice the way in which the different sexes wore this costume; hence perhaps arose the scornful saying, among the surrounding nations, that the Baganda were all women, and their inveterate habit of keeping dogs, doubtless gave rise to the still more insulting taunt, that they were the offspring of these domestic pets.

The women in mourning wore girdles of tattered green plantain leaves, perhaps an emblem of the life shattered by death, as the leaf is broken by the storm, though black people are not poetical. The struggle to obtain necessary food leaves little room for romance; and no doubt the genial current of many a noble soul is frozen at its source, which, under happier conditions, might have become a life-giving stream.

Though the king was dead and buried, the scene was not yet wholly ended. His old palace, Nabulagala, now became the "Kasubi," a kind of pale unreal image of the new king's glory and grandeur. Here at Kasubi, were old deposed chiefs, possessing the simulacra of empty titles, but without any position or influence. Their master was now a dead king, before whose tomb they did homage, yet from whom they could expect but little favour. One of the deposed chiefs was now keeper of the grave, another the spirit's "musenero," chief butler. His beer and food were regularly brought. His drum was beaten, and these living ghosts of chiefs came into the presence of the ghost of their deceased monarch, bending low before the spirit, and thus the strange pageant of giving glory to the dead is kept up.

Truly a part of the whole passionate longing of mankind to be immortal, and of that deep craving expressed in so many and such various ways, in all ages and countries, comes out here in the court and homage paid to the dead Kabaka. I ought not to say "dead," for it is not polite in Buganda to speak of the king, or other persons of position, as having died— people must say " agenze," he is gone.

Of Mutesa it is difficult to give an accurate judgment. To say he was great would be hardly true, but to say that he showed some fine qualities, and that he was, in spite of his clogging surroundings, a man who sought after better things, is to give him no more than his due

Some of his acts showed a certain breadth of view His institution of a market, and his endeavour to encourage the missionaries in bridge building, by giving them the right to levy toll on foot passengers who made use of their bridges, were indications that he wished to advance. His generally courteous treatment of all Europeans, and his forbearance, with myself for example, showed a generous spirit. I knew he disliked my intruding religion on him; I did not know the language well enough to put it in a humorous or amusing manner, even if I had possessed the wit to do so; and as Mutesa looked upon religion as an amusement and recreation, my readings about a great White Throne of Judgment, before which even kings were to stand, must have been most distasteful to the easy-going potentate. There was much that was good and loveable in him, but his education had been a training in cruelty, brutality, and lust. Such edicts as that every man was to wear a bead on his wrist, on pain of losing his head; and every woman, a bead on a string round her waist, on pain of being cut in half; such brutalities as shooting his wives, practised in his earlier days, and such vile obscenities as make daylight ashamed, which he caused to be performed in his open court, show that his training in these vices had born a plenteous crop of fearful crimes.

Some of his vilest abominations, I believe, he committed by the advice of the Arabs, but what was frequent and notorious in his unhappy successor, was seldom practised by himself. What a fearful picture was presented in reality in that gay and bright-looking palace of pleasure built upon its sunny hill!

Daily went up the terrible cries of unhappy victims, as they were deliberately hacked to pieces, with strips of reed, sharp enough to be used as knives, condemned very often for nothing, or merely for some breach of court etiquette. Frequently furnaces were smoking, in which the agonised bodies of persons, innocent of any crime, were writhing in slow torture, till death, more merciful than their tormentors, ended their anguish and despair. Sometimes scenes of hideous shame were enacted which make the heart sick to contemplate. But yet, in judging of these things, it is well to remember that there are none to whom the fearfullest crimes are not more than possibilities, for in every human heart are all these things, and out of every human heart they may proceed at any time, as He well knew, who bade His people pray, " Lead us not into temptation."

CHAPTER IX.

BEFORE proceeding to describe the new king, it may be interesting to glance at the political condition, as far as I understand it, of the Kingdom of Buganda. First, then, in order and constitutional importance, comes the divine figure of the Kabaka, or Emperor, or Czar, of Buganda. Theoretically, he is, like his Russian counterpart, an autocrat; but, like most autocrats, he is hampered on all sides by restrictions, which, in the nature of things, have arisen to limit his absolute power. He is elected on a principle which, I believe, was law in our own country in former times, namely, that the best man should be chosen, and not necessarily the eldest son of the previous king. Certain Radical politicians might, if they pleased, find in the Buganda constitution a standing protest to the world against the law of primogeniture, for, by its immemorial provision, the king's eldest son can never be king. Still, strange to say, in these revolutionary days the latest news we have from Buganda tells us that the impossible has taken place, and that the king's eldest son has been elected to the throne.

The emperor is elected by an assemblage of the great

earls, Pokino of Budu, Kangao of Bulemezi, Sekebobo of Kyagwe, Mukwenda of Singo, Kyimbugwe, keeper of the palace, Kasuju, keeper of the king's children, and possibly other principal chiefs, such as Mugema, Kibare, and Gabunga, the latter being Lord High Admiral of the king's great war canoes.

It will be simpler, perhaps, if I first try to explain how one candidate for the throne may be more likely to succeed than another. The Baganda are split up into families called Ebyika, or clans. Every Kyika (clan) has, so to speak, its distinguishing crest. There is the kyika of the grasshopper, "Ensenane;" the kyika of the sheep, "Endiga;" the kyika of the crocodile, " Engonya," and so on. It is a curious thing that no person may eat the animal after which his kyika or clan is named. The kyika of the king is the royal tribe of the Bahuma, or Balangira (princes), as they are called in Buganda. Hence we can understand how it is the Bahuma herdsmen, though utterly despised in Buganda, are yet called princes, and have the royal privilege of paring their nails to a point, and of wearing brass and copper rings upon their ankles. Strange to say, there is a rule that a man or woman must not marry in their own kyika, and marriages with cousins are viewed as marriages with sisters, and are strictly forbidden. Now every kyika presents the reigning king with one or more virgins, " Bawala," as concubines or wives, and the child of the wife given by a particular kyika to the king is that kyika's *protégé*, and consequently the candidate whom in an election the chief or chiefs belonging to that kyika are bound to support.

The king is always surrounded by his wives; and, when he is old and feeble, it is often suspected that they give him his *coup de grace*. In fact I think it is not improbable that Mutesa was smothered to death by his wives, so that polygamy, at any rate at the king's court, carries with it certain decided disadvantages.

When once the election to the throne is decided, the unsuccessful candidates are put into durance, and guarded, inside an enormous enclosure, by Kasuju, the chief appointed keeper of the king's children. In former times, it is said, the other brothers, with one or two exceptions, were put to death.

The king has his council, or "Lukiko," answering roughly to our own Privy Council, of the chiefs whom I have just mentioned, with others of less degree. He himself appoints all the chiefs, called "Aba-saza," and all the officers of his court, or "Batongole." Besides these, he appoints the under officers in the households of these chiefs. Thus these vassals, as they hold their appointments at the pleasure of the king, and not of their actual masters, are consequently largely in the power of the king; and this gives him enormous power over them, and, through them, over their masters also.

It is invariably the policy of an able Buganda king to play off one chief against another, and one party of his subjects against an opposing party. Even in dealing with foreigners, the same astute course of action has

often been followed with great success. How shrewdly
he guesses that it is the devoir of one party to counteract the teaching of heresy by the other, and of the
latter party to protest against errors. In similar
fashion, the same subtle calculation causes him to
foment and foster discord in the surrounding countries.
Then, when one party comes craving for an army to
help its particular faction, the Kabaka accedes, and
sends his horde of savage soldiers, as cowardly as
wolves, to combine with the powerful friendly faction
which he favours, and the two together can hardly fail
to conquer. Then the men, old and young, of the
defeated party are butchered in cold blood, and when
all resistance has ceased, women and children are
dragged away in numbers to a shameful and degrading
servitude.

In Buganda, as I have already stated, there are
three persons who bear the royal title of Kabaka,
namely, the king, the queen-mother, and queen-sister.
The king must always have a mother, "Namasole," and
sister, "Lubuga." If his actual mother be dead or out
of favour, another woman, probably an aunt, is chosen
to support the title. The Lubuga is chosen from the
"Bambeja," or princesses.

The Bambeja are an important body of women, often
very numerous. They are condemned to perpetual
virginity. Sometimes, however, a great chief, as a
mark of special favour, is presented with one of these
princesses for his wife. They live in some style, having

usually large grants of land, and they often own large
numbers of slaves. They are, naturally, among the
highest in the land, but, with the exception of the
Lubuga (the king's sister), have no actual official
position. The fact of their being forbidden to marry
may, by the more charitable, be looked upon as some
palliation for the scandalous lives which most of them
lead. They often use every blandishment, and even
force, to secure some young peasant, the unhappy
object of their affection ; but, should he be discovered
with them, he must meet the awful fate of death by
fire, the common capital punishment in Buganda.

Having spoken of the royal personages, the three
" Bakabaka " (sovereigns), the Balangira (princes), and
the Bambeja (princesses), I come now to the next in
order, namely, the Bakungu, or great chiefs. The
whole country is divided into five parts or earldoms—
first, Buganda proper, the district in the neighbourhood
of the king's capital, the Kibuga or Lubire ; second,
Kyagwe, to the east; third, Bulemezi, to the north-
west ; fourth, Budu, to the west ; and fifth, Singo, to the
north. These are governed by chiefs, whose titles are
the following :—Sekibobo, Earl of Kyagwe ; Kangao,
Earl of Bulemezi; Pokino, Earl of Budu; and Mukwenda,
Earl of Singo. The other great chiefs are Kymbugwe,
Mugema, and Kasuju, Kitunzi, and the admiral
Gabunga, Mutanda, Kolugi, Mujasi, and Musalo salo,
captains of the guards, and other sub-chiefs too
numerous to name.

In addition to the five earldoms, there are other official positions, appointments to which are made by the king, which confer on their holders the rank of chief—for example, the Musenero (chief butler), and Mufumbiro (chief baker whose name is Kawuta).

The under chief, the second in command in any earldom or barony, is the Mumyuka; and So-and-so is said to serve, as subordinate or Myuka, such-and-such a chief. The other offices held *by the appointment of the king* are the Sabadu, head of the slaves; Sebatimba, head of the upholsterers; Sabakaki, chief of the gate-keepers; Mutuba, chief of the bark-cloth beaters; Musali, the guide on the march; Sabagabo, &c. These are a few of the officers of a chief's household.*

The great earls themselves take honorary offices in the king's household, in this respect following the example of their European counterparts. One will be Sabadu, another Musali, and so on. The great chiefs are obliged to spend a certain number of months out of every year in waiting at the Kibuga or capital, just as the high officers of our own Queen's household. At other times they visit their provinces or chieftainships in the Kyalo, or country place. They are all feudal lords, and possess privileges analogous to those of our old feudal nobility, and are empowered to exact taxes or tribute from their numerous retainers. The

---

* In the chief's household, women sometimes hold positions of importance. The principal wife is always called the Kadu Lubare.

king has certain royal tax-gatherers, called "Basolozi," who collect brass and copper wire, bark-cloth, and cowrie shells. If, however, the people are slow to respond to the demands of these worthies, the king himself will go on a royal progress, and exact enormous benevolences from the delinquents much after the fashion of our Tudor sovereigns.

Each chief has his own drum, with its own peculiar beat, which all his vassals know. The drum is a very important feature in African political life, and in more than one county the entering on a chieftainship is expressed by the phrase, So-and-so has eaten the drum.

Pages may be found in every chief's establishment, but except in the case of the arrogant chancellor, whose pages are called "Bagala-gala," I imagine that they are merely called Balenzi (boys), and not Bagala-gala, which are an appendage of royalty.

Chieftainships are mostly hereditary, but a few, such as the Katikiro, Mukwenda, Kangao, etc., are held at the king's pleasure. Among the hereditary chieftainships are those held by chiefs of the Bataka, or landed gentry, a class of which I shall speak presently. The chiefs have absolute power of life and death in their own baronies. But any one possessing a slave may kill him for anything or nothing. I recollect Mackay telling me how a chief named Munawa killed one of his slaves for dropping a gourd of plantain cider. When Mackay pointed out to him the evil of it, old Munawa was ashamed and denied having done the

deed, and sent for another slave, who he said was the
one Mackay accused him of having killed, in order to
try and prove that he .was innocent of the crime.

The chiefs, when they go to the king's grand levee,
array themselves in their best fine cloth gold-embroidered coats and Sunday breeches. The cut of these garments would horrify a London tailor, and a missionary
who had served his apprenticeship in Bond Street would
no doubt find his vocation in Buganda. When the
chief returns from the king's presence to the bosom of
his family, he immediately doffs his finery, and betakes
himself to his graceful and comfortable " lubugu," bark-
cloth robe, and finishes the day with the help of his
"Kita," an enormous gourd of "Mwenge" (plantain
wine), which before nightfall leaves him in rather a
sottish condition.

The armies which the king sends out from time to
time to ravage the neighbouring countries are commanded by the principal chiefs in rotation. These
armies carry fire and sword, blood and iron far and
wide. Vast herds of women and cattle are swept in,
as well as thousands of children, to be from henceforth
chattels—chattels, perhaps, of children, and slaves
possibly of slaves. So miserable is their fate, so
wretched, so dulling to the senses, so destructive to all
feeling, that one can scarcely be surprised that in a few
years the unhappy creatures have given way beneath
the weight of their misery, and have even actually lost
all desire for freedom. After a raid of this kind, the

Arab, ubiquitous, heartless, bloody, finds his opportunity for buying the children and women, and is ready to purchase with his borrowed barter goods the slaves who in other countries he is able to procure more simply with his sword.

If the poor Indians at the coast are ruined by the Germans, and can no longer lend to the Arab traders, as in former times, at least some compensation may be found in the fact that it will probably result in lessening the power of the Arabs for slave-hunting; and I for one, though I sympathise with our Indian fellow-subjects, have seen too much of the bitter suffering of the victims of these Arab traders to make me regret anything which cuts off even one source of supplying them in their inhuman traffic.

The king, during his great "Barazas," will do what is termed "Give out an army" ("Gaba egye"). The chief appointed to the command is called the Mugabe. In returning home after victory, the spoil taken is divided. For the king a large proportion is set aside, and a smaller share for the chiefs and officers. The peasant soldiers often fare very badly, and what between the fearful ravages of smallpox and the frightful coughs and colds which the troops suffer from on the march, it is doubtful whether as many lives are not lost in obtaining the slaves as are gained in the influx of human spoil. Scenes of awful horror are perpetrated on these expeditions, which are unenlightened by a single ray of human kindness. Lust is lord, and wrong is right, while love is lost in the wild struggle for wealth. Illustrations might be multiplied indefinitely, but it is enough to say that it not unfrequently happens, as natives who have taken part in these raids have told me, that when some wearied woman carrying her babe is unable to keep up the rapid pace of the hurrying warriors, the child, too young and useless to be worth its carriage, is flung far into the forest, to perish with hunger or to fall a prey to some prowling hyena; while the agonised mother, when she would at all costs seek her child, is kept back and driven on by the spears of the brutal warriors.

The Bitongole are great offices under the king, and each Kitongole, as it is called, has its proper name. There is the Kilangira, so called after the princes; and the Kitesa, called after the late king. One of the Batongole* is called Namfumbambi, and always wears little bells jingling on his ankles. The origin of this practice is that a favourite of a former king was caught eaves-dropping, and his royal master humorously ordered that from henceforth his Kitongole should be distinguished by the wearing of bells, so that his inquisitive favourite should always give timely notice of his approach by his musical accompaniment.†

* " Batongole " are officers. " Bitongole " are offices.

† This story is given for what it is worth, but the practice may be derived from the Wanyamwezi, among whom the wearing of these small iron bells is very common; but, with this single exception of Namfumbambi, I never saw any one wearing them in Buganda.

A chief is buried in one of his houses, where the grave is dug, and the body is squeezed and kneaded till all the moisture is extracted, and then the mummy is wound up in strips of bark-cloth, and quantities of bark-cloth and cotton cloths are buried with the body, the amount varying according to the wealth and importance of the deceased chief.

The umbilical cord of all persons of high rank is carefully preserved, and pedigrees are kept by these relics of ancestry.

At this point I may redeem the promise I made a little while back, and say something about the Bataka or landed gentry, an important class in the country, most of whom are chiefs (Bakungu), or sub-chiefs. The Bataka, literally people of the soil, are the old landed gentry of Buganda, and are hereditary owners of the land. They are protected from eviction by the king, and may not be arbitrarily put to death by him.* Gabunga was one of these Bataka chiefs; and two other Christian sub-chiefs were also Bataka, namely the jolly old giant Kamanya, keeper of Suna's father's grave, and Kinyoro, an early though not altogether satisfactory convert to Christianity.

We now come to the second great class in the country, the Bakopi or peasants. The name Bakopi seems to be derived from a tribe who formerly came from the north

---

* The king has authority over Bataka within certain prescribed limits; he may depose one brother from the headship of the clan or chieftainship, and put another brother in his place.

of Bunyoro, Kopi, or Chopi as it is sometimes spelt,
and which Emin Pasha identifies with Shifalu. The
peasant class in Buganda are, I suppose, named from this
probably conquering people, as the slave class, Badu,
are called after the country of Budu, or Udu, as people
who only know the Swahili language usually pro-
nounce it.

The Bakopi usually attach themselves to some
"Mwami," master or chief. They have the right to
"senga," serve whom they please; and if they are
dissatisfied they have the privilege of "senguka," that
is, to leave the service of their master and attach
themselves to some one whom they fancy more. It is
not always a safe thing to do. One of my friends, a
Muhuma herdsman, who kept the Katikiro's cattle, left
the chancellor's service to enter that of the king. On
some lying pretext he was seized, his ears cut off,
and his eyes put out, as a warning that the imperious
chancellor would allow none of his servants to prefer
any one else to himself, not even the king.

The duty of the Mukopi is first to follow the chief to
war, armed with two long spears and the beautiful
shield, which the Baganda are so skilful in making.
His work at home largely consists in building houses
and making the fences which I have already described.

In return for this service, the chief will give him a
wife, and sometimes two; but she may be taken away
from him and given to his neighbour, for any or no
reason.

The Mukopi is free; but often loses his wife and children, and even his own liberty, by getting into debt, when he descends to the miserable class of Badu or slaves.

If not taken out of the country by the Arab traders, the native born slave has certain facilities for redeeming himself, and such redemption is often effected.

The sons of chiefs are in the Bakopi class, and have no recognised position in the country. Those whose mothers are of high rank are presented to the king, and also any boy remarkable for good looks or any other valuable quality.

Most of the peasants own two or three slaves. An ambitious man will quietly accumulate a number, and quarter them on his friends, who give them their scanty pittance of food for the use and show which they can make of them. Then, if their owner is given an office or Kitongole, he collects his slaves, and blossoms out with quite a train of followers behind him.

The effect of thus owning slaves, and being a hanger-on of some feudal lord, is to make these Bakopi cringing, abject, servile, and toadying to those above them, but arrogant, domineering, proud, and overbearing to those whose unhappy fate it is to be their slaves.

Lastly are the slaves, drawn, I suppose, originally from the conquered people of the country of Budu, south-west of Buganda.

How shall I speak of them?—and slavery, what can

be said of it ? The deepest degradation that strength
can inflict on weakness, the utmost depth of shame to
which an unhappy human soul can be dragged. Who
will not sympathise with those savage Bakede to
whom I have already referred, whose women's hearts
rejected with loathing the life which lay before them,
and who chose death cheerfully to being the concubines of those whom they scorned and hated ?

The slaves have no rights. What have they to do
with riches and honour, or home or hope ? Their bodies
are not their own, and the jewel of chastity, did they
ever so much desire it, lies for ever out of their
reach.

Shall we say it is well that their feelings should become so blunted that they dumbly acquiesce in their
shame ? Dare we say that because they often seem
light-hearted they do not therefore feel their own
degradation ?

The slaves in Buganda are drawn from the surrounding countries, chiefly Bunyoro and Busoga, a few
from Busàgara, Ihangiro, Buzongora, and Buzinja.
They fetch from ten thousand to twenty thousand
cowrie shells, equivalent to between three and six
pounds in English money, according to description.
A beautiful Muhuma woman will fetch far more. I
recollect one day being offered three slaves in exchange for my Muhuma boy Lugalama. The idea of
this exchange was not pleasant to me, and I replied
that, if the gentleman threw himself into the bargain,

H

I should not care even then to do business with
him.

We had a good number of little boys, some given to
us by chiefs, some sold to us.   Little Lwanga we
bought for a padlock and four yards of calico.   Some
were redeemed by us.   For instance, one of the
apprentices whom Mutesa sent to Mackay, to learn how
to work in iron, purchased a slave.   The position was
rather curious, having slaves living at an English
mission, so we had no hesitation in redeeming the boy
and setting him free.   I suppose legally we were
not justified in buying a slave even to redeem him, but
as the English law gave us no protection, and as we
were actually outlaws, we felt quite at liberty to behave
as such in particular cases of this kind.

Another little laddie, whom I christened James
Greenway, or Jimmy, I redeemed at a great price; I gave
for him a gun, a white box, a looking-glass, and a few
other things.   I used often to tell him that he had cost
far more than his market value.   When my new purchase came home, he wanted to go back to the chief who
had sold him, so I said, " All right, you shall go back in
seven days, if you wish it; if not, you can stay here."
A day or two afterwards I asked him if he wanted to
go, but the good feeding and clothes he got with us and,
I hope, kind treatment made him more than willing to
stay, and he promptly replied, " Neda Munange," " No,
my friend," " njagala kubera wano," " I want to remain
here."   I had a special interest in him, for I supposed,

though mistakenly, that he was the brother of the
boy Lugalama who was killed by Mwanga's and the
Katikiro's orders. Lugalama had told me that he had
a brother in Buganda, a slave somewhere, and I had
promised to do all I could to find him and redeem
him.

CHAPTER X.

As soon as the breath was out of Mutesa's body, the three young princes who had enjoyed their liberty by favour of the late king were at once seized and made prisoners. Of these, one, Mwanga, was to succeed Mutesa and to be future king of Buganda. Kiwewa, the eldest son, not being eligible by the custom of the country, which I have already explained, was left quietly in his own compound, little thinking that the course of events would in a few short years place him, also, on the throne of Buganda. The Council of the great Earls was summoned immediately, and deliberated under the presidency of the Katikiro, or Lord High Chancellor, while the whole country awaited with breathless expectation the result of their deliberations. After a time the sound of vociferous cheering was heard, and soon some of our friends came rushing in to us with the news: "Mwanga alide Buganda," Mwanga has eaten Buganda.*

* This metaphor of eating a drum or a country was one of the arguments sometimes used by us to demolish the doctrine of transubstantiation. It is astonishing to think that these people, who only a few years before had never heard of any one whiter than a Muhuma herdsman, should be arguing with an Englishman on the

The newly-elected king, Mwanga, at this time was a lad of some eighteen years of age. He had visited us several times, and I had tried to teach him his letters; but, wayward and flighty, he seemed unable to concentrate his attention on the same thing for any length of time. As to his moral character, there were some very evil reports current which shocked even a people so lax in morals as the Baganda.

I recollect, one day when he was paying me a visit, asking him how he would treat us if he became king? He replied, "I shall like you very much, and show you every favour." In appearance he was very like Mutesa, only shorter, and with more of the negro about him; but he lacked the common-sense and experience of his father.

The circumstances in which he was now placed may be some excuse for his subsequent tyranny, and certainly the sudden marvellous change in his condition, from a position hardly better than that of a peasant, to the autocratic authority of an African emperor, could hardly have been without deterioriating effects, and might well have turned the head of a much stronger-minded man.

---

meaning of *hoc est corpus*. As the Roman Catholic priests expressed it, it was their devoir to counteract our heresy, and they did it to such purpose that they got one or two of our converts, one especially who was most clever in argument; and on one occasion answered my objection to the Pope by asking, "How I came to have a bishop?" This was a fine handsome young chief named Bali Kudembe, who was the fourth Christian to fall a victim to the cruelty of the young tyrant who was now ruler of Buganda.

How as a god to his subjects he ruled from his
slippery eminence, and how he imbrued his hands in
innocent blood, at the cruel suggestion of the murderer
Mujasi (whose zeal for Islam at length led to his own
miserable end), until he had filled the cup of his crimes
to overflowing, and how he was as suddenly hurled
from his autocratic power as he had been suddenly
raised to it—all this makes up the terrible tragedy,
fearful scenes of bloodshed and slaughter, strange
vicissitudes of fortune which I have now to unfold.

When we first paid a visit to the new king, we
happened to arrive after the chiefs and other courtiers
had been admitted ; so, finding ourselves shut out, there
was nothing for it but to return home. The reason he
would not see us was no doubt his desire, by such
insolence, to show his sense of his new importance.
At this time we were the only white men in the
country, for the French priests had left in Mutesa's
time and had not yet returned, though they came back
some months later when Mwanga sent for them.

Mackay now left the capital and returned to finish
his work on the boat which he had been obliged to
abandon in order to superintend the burial of Mutesa.
It was a time of much rain, so "Bwana Filipo" (as Mr.
O'Flaherty was always called) and I did not again
venture to pay another visit to the king, as we thought
it better to await Mackay's return. Our enemies,
meanwhile, were busy maligning us at the court, for it
must not be forgotten that ever since our arrival we

had met with the bitterest hostility from the Arabs and from those natives influenced by them, who believed the lying slanders which the Arabs never ceased to pour into their ears.

On one occasion, indeed, during the late king's reign when Mackay brought some boxes of provisions in the boat from Musalala, the Arabs told the king that we had just received a great many loads of gunpowder, and so Mutesa sent down some of his officers to have everything examined. There was, of course, not a single ounce of gunpowder to be found; but this circumstance shows how strong even then was the feeling of suspicion against us. For in Africa it is thought a serious breach of good manners to search a stranger's private goods, and Mutesa would never have done so unless he had believed that there was sufficient ground for the gravest suspicion. Of the general causes of suspicion against white men, and against ourselves in particular, I shall speak in more detail later on.

The report which now reached the ears of King Mwanga was that Mackay was going along the coast in the boat, and was making small raids for purposes of stealing goats and plantains. As a matter of fact, the boat was beached at the time, receiving a coat of paint, and Mackay was ill with fever in his tent.

At last Bwana Filipo and I thought that we had better put in an appearance at court and tell the king ourselves how the matter really stood. Therefore, in the beginning of November, in the year

1884, we paid our first visit to the new Kabaka or emperor.

When we arrived at the king's enclosure, we were kept waiting outside for about two hours in a wretched hut where the great earls—men who are virtually kings in their own provinces—had gathered together. One of their number, Pokino, ruler of Budu, was amusing himself and the company with obscene jests. I told him it was a shame for a great man so to lower himself, and he accordingly refrained.

After we had become thoroughly tired of waiting, one of the pages came to fetch us, and we were duly ushered into the presence of our quondam pupil, now our king. It was with something of anxiety that we entered the presence-chamber of the new monarch. He was holding his court in a small house, as his new capital, or "Kibuga," had not yet been built. As we entered, he was sitting on the chair which his father had used the last time I had seen him, and looked very much like the late king. This likeness naturally helped, I believe, to determine his election; many of the chiefs wished to choose a younger boy, but the others asserted that he was not nor could not have been Mutesa's child, while of Mwanga there could be no possible doubt.*

* It sometimes occurred that as a mark of royal favour the king would send some one of his wives to a favourite chief, such as the chancellor; and, besides this, the notorious unfaithfulness of Baganda matrons made the question of paternity a doubtful and difficult one to decide.

Mwanga received us smilingly, and told us we had "kyeju"—an admirable word which perfectly depicts the character of your ordinary negro, and which includes anything between unconscious self-complacency and brazen-faced insolence. Our "kyeju," or insolence, consisted in not having sooner come to see him.

The king was dressed in Arab costume, and had a gilded mirror near him, such as may commonly be found in the front-parlours of small lodging-houses, in which he could admire his gold-embroidered vestments. In the course of conversation he praised the Arabs, our bitter enemies, and said he wished the French priests to return to Buganda, and that we must bring them. He wanted a house built for himself as well as a boat. He then asked me if I knew how to sew; fortunately I did not, or he might have set me to make him a pair of trousers. Then he inquired if I were able to make guns. He knew perfectly well that I was not, but it was his "kyeju" which made him ask these questions. Bwana Filipo and I replied that we were all three only teachers; but that, if he were willing to pay people in Europe to make these things, they would be glad to do so. The king did not like this way of putting it, so he changed the subject by asking me "if I possessed a gun." I not very wisely replied "that he had seen it when visiting us," thus reminding him that he had once been only an ordinary mortal such as ourselves.

After a little more conversation of this kind he

waved his hand, and at this signal of dismissal we
left him. The next day Mr. O'Flaherty went to see
the king in his new palace, and Mwanga at once began
begging, and made Bwana Filipo promise to give him a
field-glass which he had seen on one of his visits to the
mission.

In all the trouble and confusion of the change of
sovereigns the old chancellor had managed to keep
his place, and even called Mwanga his "mtoto," child.
The consummate art of flattery of which this ambitious
man was master was something astonishing. Mwanga
was afraid of him, and knew that the velvet paw
concealed cruel claws, and that the obsequious lord
who was ready to wipe the moisture from his face, or
to brush away a fly with a white pocket-handkerchief,
or to perform any other menial office, was in reality
his master.

Meanwhile Mackay had returned to the mission-
house, and he and I went together to pay our respects
to the Kabaka. The king had now built another temporary enclosure on the slope of Nabulagala Hill, and
quite close to Mutesa's old palace. When we reached
the entrance, we found ourselves among a turbid
swaying crowd, and our ears were deafened with the
din which a motley band of musicians were making.
Kettle-drums and hand-drums were rolling, horns
braying, flutes screaming, and the "madinda" (a
kind of dulcimer played by striking with sticks pieces
of wood arranged in a scale) gave out a not unmusical

accompaniment, while blind minstrels twanged away on their banjos, the whole making a most discordant harmony. It is the custom to put out the eyes of the court performers, as it is supposed that they will thus become more proficient in their art. There is, however, some accusation preferred against them, possibly true, but if not, no great matter : plenty of false witnesses can soon be found to represent the Crown. I have never heard of any arbitrary act of cruelty being performed in Buganda without some show of justice, even if it were only of the Star Chamber type.

Through all the noise of the other instruments we could hear the booming of the king's great drums. We made our way through an enormous crowd, till we came to the small house where the reception was being held. The king was sitting facing the door, the royal " jembe," or magic horn, a very white tusk of ivory, placed at his feet, and the chiefs in rows at each side, still dressed in mourning, that is, wearing shabby bark-cloths ; but as a mark of honour to the new king, over these were thrown rich finely-dressed skins, Mwanga himself wearing a splendid leopard-skin.

Mackay and I pushed our way to the king's presence, and sat down, one on each side before him. On entering we made polite bows, which he duly acknowledged. The uproar was tremendous, and the crowd were kneeling outside in front of the king, with their hands upon the clay ridge which surrounds the house and serves to keep out the rain. Like all Buganda houses, this one was built on the slope of a hill, with the door facing the ascent; so that this clay ridge is a very necessary precaution in case of a flood of water rushing down. This house had, however, two doors, one in front and the other at the back; ordinary people are only allowed one doorway, so that, when the king's officers come to search for delinquents, they may not escape by the back door. The crowd of sycophants were screaming for places and promotion; and I suppose here, as sometimes happens in Europe, those who screamed loudest obtained the desired posts. It was on the same principle, I imagine, that Dr. Lemuel Gulliver, in one of the countries which he visited, was informed that those who could jump the highest were thought most worthy of being ennobled. As we were jammed up in very uncomfortable positions, half crouching and half kneeling, Mackay tried to make a little more room, and unluckily happened to kneel upon the carpet on which the sacred "horn" of ivory was reposing; immediately three or four fussy chiefs eagerly warned him off. There was no intentional discourtesy in this action of theirs, for the Baganda are most particular, as indeed are all Africans, to see that their customs are strictly observed, and that the rules of etiquette are respected; so that an unhappy foreigner is almost certain to do something dreadful in their eyes. A few days before, while sitting in a house with some of the chiefs in which was one of the king's great sacred drums, I chanced to put my sun-helmet upon it; at once there was a cry of horror at the desecration, and the Earl of Bulemezi snatched it off, and handed it back to me with a reprimand. I apologised for the mistake I had unwittingly made, and so the incident terminated. In the same way I may mention that Bwana Filipo, also, while visiting the late king's tomb, chanced to turn his back upon the grave, and so incurred a sharp rebuke from the chief in charge for insulting the deceased Kabaka, whose spirit was there. So much do they hold the idea of reverence to a deceased monarch, that every chief who received any promotion was obliged after saying "neanze, neanze," etc., to the three Kabakas, the king and his mother and sister, to go and "Kweanza" before the tomb of the late king. These instances will serve to show how easily, from ignorance, a stranger may give offence. The people of Buganda, however, had the good sense and delicate feeling to pardon errors that we frequently made which would have met with severe punishment and fines, had their own people committed them. Other tribes will make a breach of custom an excuse for exacting a heavy fine. I recollect when travelling in the Usukuma country, south of the Nyanza, one of our party shaved his head. The people assured us that this was "mwiko," or unlawful, since they had not yet sown their corn; it was most annoying, if slightly amusing. But they made him pay ten cloths, or forty yards of unbleached calico, for the breach of custom.

But to return—the present public " baraza," or reception, did not last long, for Mwanga got up suddenly
and retired; presently he sent a page to call the
Katikiro, or chief judge, Mackay, and myself to a
private interview. We were conducted through
several reed-built courts, until we came to another
small house where the king received us. We found
him lying on the ground stretched upon some rich
carpets obtained from the Arabs. The old king
Mutesa used always to allow the Katikiro and other
honoured guests to sit inside the house with him; but
this young Rehoboam had no such intention, so we
were all stationed in the doorway. My stool happened
to be nearer him than Mackay's; he bade us change
places, and then the conversation began. Mackay was
chief speaker. In front of the king was his favourite
large mirror, while he held a small one in his hand.

Mwanga was inclined to be self-willed and rude,
while Mackay was perfectly polite and firm. " Do
you want to go to Musalala (at the south of the Lake)
to bring more white men?" said the king. " No,"
replied Mackay, " but if you wish it I will go." " Very
well," rejoined the King, " I will give you a 'mubaka'"
(messenger), and he named Kadu Mayanja, a man
whom Mackay knew well, a turbulent and murderous
character. Mackay said " he did not wish this person
to accompany him; would the king appoint some one
else?" " Oh, I see," said Mwanga, " you think he is
too clever, and that is the reason you do not like him."

Mackay said, " Give me Bijugo," "little bells," this was the king's confidential page. Bijugo, however, modestly said that his "magezi," "cleverness," was not equal to that of Kadu Mayanja, to which the king, and consequently the company, assented. Mackay replied by saying, "Very well, if Kadu Mayanja is so clever, he can go by himself with the boat, and I will remain behind." Mwanga then gave way, and called Sematimba Michah, one of his Christian pages, who afterwards became a sub-chief, and appointed him to go with Mackay. After a good deal more desultory talk, we were dismissed, having formed not too favourable an opinion of our new ruler.

CHAPTER XI.

THERE is an old prophecy current in Buganda that the country is to be conquered by a people coming from the East. How strongly this idea seems to have possessed the people may be seen in the jealousy with which they tried to keep strangers from going in that direction. Mutesa said to Mackay when the subject of a direct easterly route was mooted between them: "I know you white men want exceedingly to see what there is beyond Busoga, but I will never permit it." Possibly this astute monarch feared that his ivory preserves would eventually be tapped by the agency of Europeans, and that the Busoga ivory would find an outlet other than through Buganda.

It is therefore not a matter of surprise that the Baganda people and their rulers should look with suspicion upon the advent of foreigners so unlike any people whom they had ever seen before; nor that our teaching and the marvellous influence which that teaching gave us should be viewed with suspicion and dislike by those in power.

Our methods seemed to them as contemptible as dangerous. We were willing to teach "balenzi" and "badu," boys and slaves, and with dismay they saw the very flower of their nation and the young aristocrats who would hereafter be powerful chiefs flocking about us, and hanging upon our words and eagerly reading our books. Sebwato, the Katikiro's most trusted sub-chief, and Mayanja, lately a powerful chief and still keeper of Kamanya's (Mutesa's grandfather) grave, were openly baptized, while in no short time many chiefs, of whom the most powerful was the boy-admiral Gabunga, followed their example.

Had the royal personages and chiefs known what we knew of the tremendous new power which had entered their country, they would have agreed with the adversary quickly while in the way with him; but of this they had yet much to learn. They could see indeed a dim danger ahead looming fearfully in the distance, but they knew not how to meet it. It is merely a truism to say that mankind are universally actuated by self-interest, a fact in human nature which the Divine Teacher recognised, and to which He made His appeal.

But of any interests beyond the present, and of any gain besides that of wealth or comfort or power, the Baganda had no conception, any more than the fanatical Arabs, who never tired of telling them that we were simply agents of the British Government.

Unfortunately the Arabs thoroughly believed this themselves, and therefore they spoke with that sincere conviction which only a belief in their own statements could give; and hence the coming of white men

I

in response to the invitation given by King Mutesa through Stanley in 1875 could only be viewed by that ruler and his counsellors as an advent for some interested purpose, a purpose which to their eyes became more and more evidently that of seizing upon the country. It will be seen that there were many circumstances, slight in themselves and insignificant, which, when taken together and viewed through the medium of native fears, heightened by Arab hostility, combined to give colour to the growing suspicions entertained by the rulers of Buganda.

The arrival of white men was particularly grievous to the Arabs, who looked upon us as possible rivals in trade as well as actual rivals in religion, and who believed that one of our main objects was to thwart their paramount interest, the slave trade.

It was indeed natural that we should be looked upon as direct agents and representatives of our country, since the white men of whom the Baganda had any knowledge were rulers and governors—Baker, Gordon, Emin. Moreover, the gradual encroachment of Egypt from the north with her powerful white pashas was a constant source of alarm to the Baganda people. Buganda was indeed for a while occupied by Egyptian troops, and theEgyptian flag was hoisted by their leader almost under Mutesa's nose. Gordon Pasha removed these troops, and I am under the impression that one of Emin Pasha's visits to Buganda was for this purpose. We were told that when the Egyptian leader came to visit Mutesa, the king brought some hundreds of his "bagazi" (gate-keepers) and "bamboa" executioners, and ordered that a couple of them should stand behind each Egyptian soldier, and on the least sign of hostility they should attempt to bind the Egyptian troops. Great fires were kept burning all night through, and the whole country was on the alert, awaiting an attack.

When the first missionaries arrived (under the leadership of Shergold Smith—than whom no braver man has set foot in Africa) in June 1877, they presented to Mutesa a letter of introduction from the English Foreign Secretary, and also a letter from the Church Missionary Society, signed among others by the Archbishop of Canterbury. Whether the missionaries made clear to Mutesa who or what the Archbishop was, I very much doubt. But these letters naturally could only have given the King of Buganda one impression, namely that the bearers of them were ambassadors of the Queen of England. There were in addition always present hostile Arabs with their explanations of such credentials.

The next advent of missionaries was by way of the Nile in 1879, when Mr., now the Rev. Charles Pearson, the Rev. G. Litchfield, and Mr., now Dr. Felkin, were enabled to reach their destination by the generous kindness of General Gordon, who provided them with an Egyption escort, and commanded all the "Vakeels," or governors of the various stations, to treat them with every consideration. Mutesa had sent some of

I 2

his people north, who naturally concluded that the mission party was a political embassy, and told the king on their return that the "Bangereza" (Englishmen) were bringing him a large present from the Queen. When the party reached Buganda with their baggage, which looked like untold wealth to the ignorant people of Buganda, Mutesa sent down messengers to ask for the gift from his friend Queenie, whose people the new-comers were. Still further to increase the already strong conviction as to the direct relation between the missionaries and the Government, Mr. Pearson's party produced a letter from the Foreign Office, recommending them to the favour of the King of Buganda.

Her Majesty's Consul at that time in Zanzibar apparently considered that, perhaps unconsciously, the missionaries were giving native rulers the impression that they were accredited agents of the British Government, in which it is obvious from what I have already said he was perfectly correct. I do not think the missionaries were necessarily to blame, nor do I think that the Consul in Zanzibar blamed them; but I think I am correct in saying that he wrote to Mutesa, telling him that he was the only accredited agent of her Majesty in Eastern Equatorial Africa. On receipt of this letter Mutesa at once accused the missionaries of presenting bogus letters, and of being impostors. The missionaries in turn wrote home to complain to the committee of their society that their position was a false and unpleasant one, and pressure was apparently brought to bear upon the Consul at Zanzibar by the Church Missionary Society, so that he wrote to Mutesa the following letter :—

"H.B.M. Agency and Consulate-General,

"Zanzibar, Nov. 24, 1879.

"To King Mutesa of Uganda.

"Sir,—The directors of the Church Missionary Society in England, by whom Messrs. Wilson, Mackay and others now with you were sent, have received reports from these gentlemen to the effect that their lives have been endangered in consequence of letters which, they say, I wrote to you, stating that no Englishman in Uganda came from the Queen, or had letters from the English Government. I am directed if this be correct to write and explain that the letters presented were given to the missionaries by the English Government.

"Your Majesty knows that what has been reported is not correct, and I have the best reason to be satisfied that so far from these gentlemen's lives being in danger, they were, long after my letters reached and up to a recent date, well received and in favour at your court. In proof of which your Majesty had allowed some of your people to accompany one of them to Europe.

"As to a letter addressed to your Majesty by the Marquis of Salisbury, dated May, 1878, I have to inform you that, on receiving a copy thereof, fearing the original might be delayed, I wrote and explained its contents, in order that you might be encouraged to extend to the missionaries the protection and assistance you had already shown to all Europeans. I have only now to repeat what I have said, and ask your Majesty to encourage and protect all travellers, traders, and missionaries who may visit your dominions, and to allow one and all of them to travel where they please, and to leave the country, should they wish to do so, by any route they may select, either by way of the Nile or Unyamwezi, or by any new route they may have a mind to try.

"I have the honour to be,

"Your Majesty's most obedient humble servant,

(Here his signature),

"H.M. Agent and Consul-General."

This letter shows so admirably the state of muddle which had now been reached, that, at the risk of being tedious, I have given it in full. Reference is here made to the envoys brought to England from Buganda by Messrs. Felkin and Wilson. Their idea in persuading Mutesa to send some of his people to Europe was that such a visit would do more than anything else to give the Baganda people a better knowledge of their relation to the outside world. Had Messrs. Felkin and Wilson been able to prevail upon Mutesa to send some of his chiefs or superior officers, the experiment might have proved a success; as it was, Mutesa sent some utterly insignificant people of the "Bakopi," or peasant class. Long afterwards, when speaking of this to Mackay, he said, "You Bazungu, white men, can make many wonderful things, but my 'magezi gezi,' cunning, is much superior to yours. Did I not send some slaves to Bulaya, Europe, and did the Bazungu not believe them to be chiefs?"

The fact that the two missionaries undertook to conduct the King of Buganda's envoys to England, with the letter which Mutesa wrote to Her Majesty, naturally gave them, in Mutesa's view, the appearance of being the accredited agents of the Queen, and although Her Majesty only received the envoys at a private audience, and the Foreign Office refused to receive them officially, it was quite enough for Mutesa to know that his messengers had been received and his presents accepted by the august woman-ruler who held sway in Bulaya.

The further fact that Mutesa's messengers were brought back to Buganda in charge of a missionary, who was the bearer of return presents to the King of Buganda, and of a letter from the then Foreign Secretary, must have removed any little lingering doubt from the mind of the people of Buganda that the white English missionaries were, or could be, anything else but direct agents of the British Government.

It was only natural and right that the British Consul-General at Zanzibar should wish to keep up friendly relations with so important a native ruler as Mutesa, and, to secure this end, he corresponded with the King of Buganda, sending him occasional presents.

When Mutesa died, the Consul wrote to congratulate Mwanga upon his accession. Subsequently I wrote to our Consul to ask him to write and explain to Mwanga what we really were, a request to which he promptly and courteously acceded.

The Consul-General's position in the matter was somewhat difficult, since I asked him to do what he had been apparently blamed by other missionaries for having done some time previously; nevertheless, he wrote distinctly to Mwanga, telling him that we were only teachers of religion and nothing more.

We were the only Englishmen in Buganda at the time, and he requested us to ask Mwanga to forward letters which he sent with our mail to Emin Pasha. We were thus the natural channel of communication between the beleaguered pasha in the north and the east coast, and so the suspicion which had hardly slumbered was again awakened, that we were in league with the dreaded "Batuluki" (Egyptians) from the north.

Rumours of troubles in which Bazungu played a prominent part reached Buganda from all quarters. In the north there was news of fighting in the Soudan in which the English were implicated; news of German annexations in the east; news, uncertain, undefined, of Bazungu advancing from the west, and the advent of English missionaries and German traders in the region south of the Nyanza made the outlook in all directions stormy and uncertain. Mr. Thomson had suddenly appeared in Busoga, and had as suddenly retired. He had sent no present and no message to Mutesa, who died shortly afterwards.

But the news of Thomson's coming, distorted and magnified by the terrors of the narrators, together with the other circumstances already mentioned as operating to make us objects of fear and suspicion was, I think, the immediate cause of the terrible tragedy which I shall relate in the succeeding chapters, and of which two young Christian lads especially dear to me were the first innocent victims.

CHAPTER XII.

LUGALAMA.

WHEN Rumanika, King of Karagwe, died, the succession was disputed between two of his sons. One of these, Entare, "the lion," sent to Mutesa and obtained his help. By means of a Baganda army, supplemented by his own faction, Entare overcame his brother, who took refuge on an island in the lake Mwutanzige (?). The supporters of the conquered brother were handed over to the tender mercies of the Baganda raiders, who swept the country far and wide, and so, by means of the swords of their own tribe, managed to enslave a large number of the lighter-coloured Bahuma. While this raid was proceeding, the news reached the zereba where Lugalama's father and mother lived that a Baganda war-party was close at hand, and they could hear the sound of the hostile drums as the raiders came on to the attack. Immediately there was a hurried flight of women and children. Soon the Baganda came up. The Bahuma men could only fight and die (for there is no quarter given in African warfare), and then there only remained the easy task of hunting out the spoil. Lugalama and his little brother ran and hid themselves in the long canes, and soon,

with breathless horror, they heard the yelling of the
painted warriors close at hand beating the long
grass. Soon the children were spied and dragged out.
The thirst of blood is on their cruel captors, and they
cry, "Kill the bigger one, kill him!" A spear is
raised—but a darker fate awaited him. These raids
showed only the brute man with cruelty not yet re-
fined and hardened by the dogmas of a fanatical
religion. Lugalama was yet to learn more of the
wickedness of the world and to be mocked and taunted
and slowly tortured to death on account of a creed of
which he could hardly judge. At this time, however,
a chief, Sebwato by name, came up and seized him,
bidding his would-be murderers begone. He, good
man, snatched the little charms, "ensiriba," the child
was wearing about his neck and flung them away. He
had already thrown away his own, for he had begun to
learn at our Mission. He was a superior man and
very kind-hearted, and afterwards became one of my
warmest friends. For the present he took his little
prize and tied his hands, and the march back was
begun. The mother was seized by some one else, the
other children by others. Thus this peaceful little
family was broken up and ruined, and its members
separated to go away into slavery and shame, and this
child to a cruel, lingering death.

Sebwato gave him some small thing to carry, but it
was very burdensome to him, for he could not eat
the new kind of food which they gave him. The

Bahuma, like the Masai, live entirely upon milk, and now no milk could be obtained, only scanty supplies of sweet potatoes and plantains. Many of the little children perished on this pitiful march. If they survived, what lay before them ? To be bandied about from owner to owner, at last, most likely, to fall into the hands of the most abject of the sons of men—the mongrel descendants of slave-dealing Arabs, or Arabs themselves almost as low.

And so the caravan of captive women and children went on, leaving the Kagera River behind choked with the corpses of husbands and brothers who had died in their defence, the way marked by the emaciated bodies and whitening bones of helpless children who died on the terrible march. This is Africa left to herself. Livingstone, Stanley, and Cameron have told us what Africa is when left to the Arabs. If such recitals as these have any meaning, it is that the most powerful appeal is made to civilised nations to take the African tribes under their fostering care. It is an appeal to England to do for Africa what she has so triumphantly effected for the peoples of India.

Sebwato, Lugalama's captor, sent him on before with a part of his following, but when the boy reached Buganda he was quickly kidnapped from his new owner ; but Mugaju or Lugalama, having appreciated the kindly disposition of Sebwato, managed to escape from his kidnappers and return to his first captor. Now Sebwato had determined to set the child free, and

show his appreciation of the teaching he had received
at the Mission by sending him to us. He knew
that we hated slavery, and thus his sending him
to the Mission was practically manumitting him.
There were not wanting mischievous boys who told
Lugalama (Mugaju, as his new master called him)
that the white men were most cruel, and would
certainly cut off his ears. This horrible practice is so
common in Buganda that the child might well believe it
possible. I remember the first day that he came with
his master to our house. He was dressed in ragged
bark cloth, but not even rags could make him look
common. I was at once struck by his face, so different
from the other followers of the chief. When he came
to live with us he soon showed himself quick at
learning. At first he wished to return to his first captor
(the story of the cutting off ears was, I think, haunting
his mind), but he soon learnt that this was untrue,
and lost his fear of the strange-looking Bazungu
(Europeans). I remember that some time afterwards
Sebwato came and told me that the boy belonged to
one of the chief families of Karagwe, and that the King
Entare wanted to get him back again. I said I did not
think it right to keep him from those who had so
strong a claim upon him, if he wished to return to
them. Lugalama was listening to this conversation, and
when Sebwato had gone he came up to me and said
" Do not agree to what he says, they only want to take
me back to sell me to the Arabs." This boy was one

of the few Africans I have met with who seemed really
to care much for his parents. He told me the story of
his capture, and when I asked him about his father
he could hardly speak, and his beautiful eyes filled
with tears at the thought of his death.

Speaking of the sensibilities of Africans, it may be
worth while to relate that when I was last at Usambiro,
at the south of the Nyanza, there was a young
Muhuma, whom the Katikiro had given to Mackay for
doing some work for him. This little fellow's name
is Ndongolc, or Timoteo. I had given an order
to kill a sheep which was ailing, in order to save it
from dying a lingering death, when Ndongole, or
Kayima, as we always called him, who was standing
by, began to whimper and cry. "What on earth is the
matter with you ?" I asked him; and he said, " I am so
sorry for its little lamb, which will be left an orphan."
I immediately, though perhaps weakly, reprieved the
poor sheep, which, however, died in a day or two, but
I could not resist such eloquent pleading.

Mugaju Lugalama soon became a great friend of
mine, and was a general favourite. On one occasion,
when Mackay and I visited the Katikiro, he came with
us, and the Chancellor's eye immediately fell upon the
handsome Muhuma boy, and he asked who he was, and
how we had got him ; and when we said he had been
given us by Sebwato the Katikiro seemed displeased
and vexed, but let the matter drop. At the time we
suspected nothing, but we discovered afterwards that the

chief was annoyed that we should receive gifts of boys, as if we were chiefs, forsooth! I mentioned in a former chapter the practice of sending pages to the king and powerful chiefs. About the time of Lugalama's coming to us we were visited by a large number of the king's pages who were learning to read, and among others two who deserve especial mention, Mukassa, who was named Samweli, and Kakumba, named Yusufu. Kakumba always took much interest in our teaching, and was very fond of coming to see us. After a time his master died, and he told us that he wished to come and serve, "senga," us. This we allowed. Now people only go to "senga," *i.e.* serve, a chief or person of authority in the country, and our allowing young men and boys to stay at the Mission gave the chiefs, who were always listening to the slanders of Arab enemies and others, the impression that we wished to gain a position of power and influence in the country by attaching a number of followers to ourselves. Kakumba was a very religious boy, and, though somewhat weak, was a very willing and obedient scholar and servant. Mukassa, whom I first knew as the "guava boy," was a very nice gentlemanly little page. He used always, unlike the usual run of visitors, to bring a little present of guavas, or "mapera"* as the fruit is called in Buganda.

* "Mapera" was the name by which the French priests were always called. When they were first asked their names they replied, "Mon père," and the Baganda immediately made it into the word most like a word with which they were familiar.

Mukassa was a most eager and anxious little learner, and I soon gave him our small first lesson-book, containing the Lord's Prayer, Ten Commandments, and Scripture texts. A day or two afterwards Mr. O'Flaherty met him in great tribulation, and found that poor Mukassa had lost his book, and was in deep grief about it. I comforted him by giving him another copy. He and many more candidates were baptized the following Christmas Day, when we had a great feast; and this was magnified by our enemies into a seditious gathering. I have indicated in previous chapters other occurrences such as this, which, though small in themselves, taken together, helped to strengthen the growing suspicions entertained against us. How these suspicions led to a terrible calamity I shall tell in the next chapter.

Mwanga had not long been on the throne of Buganda before he began to show himself in his true colours He constantly kept sending down to the Mission for things he wanted, and asked Mackay to make him a lightning conductor for the top of the vast straw-built house in which Mutesa was buried. These demands, however, upon our property and our time were but precursors of worse treatment which we were to receive. We were getting on well with teaching and printing, but evil rumours of coming ill were thick in the air. The name of the Mission was Natéte, a pretty English-looking house on the sloping side of a hill, a ravine below, banana groves all about us. A broad road ran past our own garden fence, opposite this road was an old fellow named Gomera, whose dependents robbed us on the right hand, while another set of people robbed us on the left, and at the back an Arab had a number of slaves who partly lived on what we cultivated. This Arab, Hamisi by name, was a friendly old fellow, and had formerly supplied one of our missionaries with food and cloth when he was in great extremity. He was but a very lax follower of Islam, and not a little given to the bottle. Later, he offered an asylum to some of our terrified little Mission boys when the murderers were abroad.

Immediately above us lived Bugalla, a great friend of Sebwato's and consequently of ours. He had a curious history, which he related to me one day. When Bugalla was quite a little boy, Mutesa had determined to become a Mahometan, and so the whole country was set to work at the Koran; the king's pages were circumcised by the score, as well as many others, and Islam looked triumphant; and poor Lubare, the divine guide of the Baganda, was for a time in the background. But one of the holy and important points of Islam is, that every animal that is killed for food should be turned towards the sacred city Mecca, and that the slayer must be circumcised. Now the functionary who killed the king's beef happened not to have embraced the belief in the prophet, and consequently did not kill his beasts in the orthodox way, and hence the Baganda Mahometans could not now, and (to their credit be it said) *would* not

K

eat the defiled meat of the king; and when the haughty
tyrant sent them beef of his own cattle, they more
haughtily refused it.   Now they knew one whose words
were weightier even than the Kabaka's.   When
Mutesa heard it he was troubled, and all Buganda with
him, and soon the awful edict went forth that every
follower of Islam was to die.   Then there was a
sickening scene of ruthless slaughter, and a strict
search was made for every one who had the damning
evidence of his having accepted the new belief.
Bugalla managed to hide, and so to evade the in-
quisitors.   Soon, as was always the case in Buganda, the
storm spent itself, but Islam had received a blow from
which it has not yet recovered.   Bugalla afterwards
became a chief, and finally was created Kyimbugwe,
keeper of the palace, by Kiwewa, the monarch who
succeeded Mwanga.   How he afterwards behaved to
the missionaries, and how he met his death, must be
related in a subsequent chapter.

Another of our neighbours was the boy-chief Gabunga,
who was a regular attendant at the Mission and a
thorough little gentleman.   Though he was one of the
biggest chiefs in the country, he was quite simple and
unaffected.   He, alas, later on met with a tragic fate.

Before new dangers arose, we had just passed through
a time of trouble in a terrible visitation of the small-
pox.   This frightful malady, and the plague, a kind of
"black death" called "kaumpuli," from time to time
decimate the population of Buganda.   Kaumpuli is

recognised by the swellings in the armpit and in the groin, and by a terrible rise in the temperature of the patient. The fever runs its course in about twenty-four hours, and usually proves fatal.

Small-pox perhaps kills more people, yet it is not so much feared by the natives as kaumpuli, of which they have the greatest terror, as it is supposed to be frightfully infectious.

Speaking of the kaumpuli, I may refer to an incident recorded in the admirable book containing Emin Pasha's letters. Emin describes a conversation which he held with the Baganda guides who led him to Mutesa's capital. He asked them why Mwambia's land was totally depopulated. They replied that there was in Uganda a powerful magic called "Kampódi"—no doubt this very "kampoli" or "kaumpuli." The letters *r*, *l* and *d* are under certain conditions interchangeable in the Lake languages.

The mistake which follows is, though very natural, a little amusing. Emin, believing the magic spoken of to be simply one of Mutesa's notorious raids, asked the guides if it affected goats and cows or household utensils, "and both gentlemen were silent." If an intelligent Chinee were to ask us if the measles affected our silver spoons we should perhaps hardly be so polite as to keep a reserved silence. Emin draws the conclusion that Mutesa always enveloped his plundering expeditions in a veil of mystery.

To return to this epidemic of small-pox, "kawali,"

Mr. O'Flaherty's attendant, a young married Christian, was the first to fall sick, and he had the disease in the most virulent confluent form. When I visited him I saw that he had all that he wanted, but asked if he needed anything more. He beckoned me to come near, and then said, "I want you to pray with me." This man was never forsaken by his faithful wife, who tended him all through his loathsome disease until his death, though he had been often unfaithful to her.

Soon another boy was attacked, then a woman, then Lugalama showed unmistakable symptoms of the dread disease. We removed the patients, five in all, to a good-sized house which had been formerly occupied by one of the missionaries. An old woman, together with the wife of one of our converts, and a little Munyoro girl, who was a source of constant trouble on account of her bad behaviour, and the two boys, made up the complement of the sick. During this critical time Mackay was away, and I had to become sick-nurse. Poor little Lugalama became quite light-headed and delirious, which my companion assured me was a certain sign that he would die. The poor boy was filled with the idea that one of the women patients was going to bewitch him and so cause his death. However, she did not succeed in doing so, and they all made a good recovery.

After this somewhat lengthy digression I return to the rumours of coming ill which were now gaining strength. The king at this time expressed a wish for

a box, so I took him a long white tin box, which I first
neatly lined with white paper. My friend Kakumba
went with me to the royal enclosure to carry it.
I was admitted into Mwanga's presence, and I heard
the king give a quiet order to the executioners. Then
he looked at the box. He was polite enough, but said he
wanted a different kind, so I said we would look for
another of the sort he preferred. I then took my
leave. On coming to the door I found poor Kakumba
in a state of great terror, saying, "My friend, they are
going to seize me." I tried to reassure him, and
passed out, while he almost clung to me. When I
got home I found that orders had actually been given
to seize all followers of ourselves and the Arabs.
Immediately there was a stampede, and Kakumba and
other Baganda left us. I did not credit the rumour
myself, and thought it only an idle scare; however,
Lugalama came to me, and, taking my hand, said, "My
friend, you do not understand Luganda;* Mwanga did
give orders to seize Kakumba."

In the beginning of 1885, Mackay had arranged
that he would go down with the boat to Musalala, at
the south end of the Nyanza, and take our letters
but first he had to go up to Mwanga to obtain per-
permission. When he was admitted he asked the king
to give him the required leave; but Mwanga told him
he must bring back a white man, which Mackay refused to do. The king then asked him if he wanted

* Luganda is the language of Buganda.

a messenger, to which Mackay replied that he did not. We wanted to be able to come and go when we pleased, and to send the boat when we wished, without Mwanga's messengers being on board. Mackay did not of course say this, but remarked that Baganda could not comfortably eat the food that was supplied to the boat's crew, who were Zanzibaris. The king then said he might go; but this trifle light as air confirmed his suspicions already aroused by busy slander, and a page was at once despatched to the Katikiro privately, telling of Mackay's refusal to take a messenger. Our position was now most difficult, as we were working quite in the dark, and dealing with people who could not be straightforward, and who never believed what we said.

The king then bade Mackay to go to the Katikiro, the haughty chancellor, to obtain his permission as well. To him accordingly Mackay applied, and this arch-hypocrite and murderer, this crafty, clever, subtle, smiling master of dissimulation received him blandly and politely. He gave him the required leave, and actually sent a slave to bring a couple of goats as food for the voyage which he had already made up his mind that Mackay should not take. Mackay returned to us in the evening and packed up the things that he required for the journey. I intended to accompany him to the lake to see him off, and to spend the next day with him on the Nyanza. Kakumba and Lugalama, my two faithful young followers, were to come with me.

While writing letters late at night we heard the beating of war drums and wondered what it could mean, since we had heard of no contemplated raid, yet it sounded as if an army were being collected. As I went to bed I passed the ante-room where Lugalama, and Benjy and Lwanga, two other little freed slaves, slept. I shall never forget how I stopped to look at Lugalama's peaceful sleeping face. Though one can hardly believe in presentiments, I somehow felt the shadow of an overhanging calamity from which I could not free myself. I held the candle above him. How still he is—how quietly he sleeps—how like sleep is to death! He moans uneasily, dreaming perhaps of his murdered father, or his mother worse than dead. And so good-night, young Lugalama—for the last time good-night.

CHAPTER XIII.

DEATH OF LUGALAMA.

THE next morning was to be an eventful one for us. Soon everything was ready, and our little party started for the lake. Our caravan consisted of the crew of the boat, and three or four boys besides Lugalama and Kakumba, while Mackay and I brought up the rear. One of our friends called Paulo and one or two other of the native Christians accompanied us on the way. A rumour reached us that the Mahometan chief Mujasi (the miserable Sawaddu who proved such a coward and miscreant in his dealings with H. M. Stanley, and who is mentioned in that traveller's account of his visit to Uganda) was out with a large armed following. Paulo and his companions, fearing some danger, bade us a hasty farewell and departed, but we kept on our journey. As we walked along we saw every now and then men armed with shields and spears hurrying past us as if hastening to some rendezvous. We called one of the warriors and asked him where these soldiers were going. He looked a little confused, but replied that some of the king's women had run away, and that they were going in pursuit of them. Mackay lingered a little in order to get some bearings with his compass, and thus we were left pretty far behind the rest of our party. As we neared the lake and were about to enter a tangled forest, which lay between us and the Nyanza, an armed throng suddenly confronted us, headed by Mujasi himself, wearing a dirty old pair of European trousers and a shabby coat. I did not know that this miserable-looking object was a Muganda chief, although he carried a long sword. The armed men pressed upon us and blocked the way, crying out, "Go back! go back!" ("Mudeyo! mudeyo!"). We replied, "We are the king's friends, we have received the king's leave. How do you dare to insult the king's guests?" and we attempted to proceed. On this we were rudely hustled, and the sticks which we were carrying were in eager terror snatched from our hands. Mackay and I offered no resistance, but went and sat quietly down at the side of the path. Our enemies grew bolder; soon they seized us and pulled us to our feet. Mackay simply allowed them to carry him for a little distance, while I walked slowly on. Then Mackay regained his feet, and we were dragged and pushed along for some distance, a guard of five or six men placing themselves between the two terrible-looking Bazungu. After a while, when they saw we offered no resistance, they allowed us to walk quietly together, and we heard them commend our prudence in going so peaceably. We now asked the men to let us see the leader, and when he came we offered him a present to let us go quietly on our way. When we had proceeded some eight miles on our return to the capital (Mengo), we came to a point where two roads met, one leading straight to Mengo, and the other more to the left to Natéte, our Mission headquarters. Here we were halted, and soon our porters and boys, who were behind, came up. The boat's crew were free, though their guns had been taken from them, but our Mission boys all had their hands tied. When I saw my little Muhuma friend with his hands bound, without thinking, I went straight to him and began to undo the cord. It was, I am afraid, a most foolish proceeding on my part, in the face of the armed and angry soldiers. Their leader seized his sword and seemed beside himself with fury. He had lost all self-control, and danced and brandished his weapon in my face, crying out, "You're drunk! You're drunk!" "I am not drunk," I replied. In my excuse it must be remembered that I did not know that this wretched-looking creature was in reality a powerful chief, and so, standing perfectly still, I scornfully added, "Come with your sword, you slave." This was too much for Mujasi's dependents, and they began to push me violently, though no blow was struck. Mackay tried to come to me, but the loaded guns of the soldiers were thrust before him, so he called out, "Come away." I turned and went towards him, and saw the sorrowful face of poor little Lugalama for the last time on earth. The word was given, and still guarded, we resumed our march. After a while, when we had come to another road that led to Natéte,

we were bidden to go back to our own house, and the
Mujasi and his triumphant guards marched on to
Mengo, the king's enclosure. Mackay and I sat down
to consider our position. It was about three o'clock
in the afternoon, and we had been hustled and marched
under guard for the last two hours and a half, besides
the two or three hours' walk towards the Nyanza before
our arrest, and we were very weary and despondent.
The Rubicon had at length been passed by Mwanga's
insolent soldiers, and the terror with which we, as
Bazungu (white men), had hitherto been regarded,
seemed to have disappeared. Now, the Baganda could
see that we were merely helpless mortals, and that it
would be an easy matter to make an end of us. Truly
this was a serious crisis for us, but it consoled us to
think that we had not suffered this insulting treatment
by the order either of the king or the Katikiro, though
we found out later our delusion on this point. We
decided to lose no time, but to lay the whole matter
at once before the Katikiro. When we reached his
enclosure we were bidden to wait. A few Arabs were
sitting in one of the houses, and we joined them.
They were of course discussing what was now the most
absorbing topic, for the news had spread rapidly
through the country that the Bazungu had been en-
trapped by Mujasi. No one dared to announce our
presence to the Katikiro, as Mujasi was having a private
interview with him, reporting his success in the late
encounter. After waiting some time, we got up and

went to the doorway, and Mackay called out loudly,
'Katikiro, my friend, I am your friend. We are the
white men." After calling once or twice we were
admitted and invited inside the house, and Mackay
stated our case and asked why we had been so badly
treated. To our surprise the judge rather defended
Mujasi, and wanted to know the meaning of Mackay's
having threatened him with his gun. As Mackay
had had no gun, and as the stick he was carrying had
been immediately wrested from him, he simply replied
that it was false. The judge then asked what we
meant by taking Baganda out of the country. Again
Mackay explained that Kakumba, the only Muganda
in the party, was carrying my mat, and that he was
not going in the boat. The subject was then dropped,
and another case came on for hearing. When this was
disposed of, Mackay returned to our affair, and told the
chancellor that it was a bad thing to treat guests as
we had been treated. The judge listened, but said
little. However, as Mackay proceeded, the chancellor's lips were tightly compressed, and suddenly
with flashing eyes he turned to Mujasi and said, " Take
the Bazungu (Europeans) and send them away, and let
them return no more." This was a terrible blow, and
we sought now in vain to deprecate the great man's
wrath. His anger grew, or he made it appear to grow,
more fiery, and calling Mujasi forward, he said with
suppressed passion, " See, Mujasi, dress yourself to-
morrow, and seize Mackay and Filipo, and this one,"

pointing to me, "and bind them and send them and all
their things out of my country, and return them to
Bulaya (Europe)." Immediately Mujasi arose, and his
men with him, and seizing long reeds, they went
through evolutions as if attacking an imaginary foe
with spears, while they shouted, "Neanze, neanze ge."
Mackay and I were utterly taken aback and astounded·
at this decision, and we begged the chancellor to hear
us and tried to take his hand to plead once more.
But he waved us scornfully aside, and, with a cry of
triumph from Mujasi's soldiers, we were hustled and
dragged from the great man's presence, a dangerous
and angry mob momentarily growing thicker about us.
Soon they were actually quarrelling for our clothes.
"Mine shall be his coat," shrieked one; "Mine his
trousers;" "No, mine!" and there was a scuffle to get
nearer the clothing they coveted. However, the chancellor did not wish matters to go quite so far, and sent
his head executioners to warn off the vulture soldiers.
The order was instantly obeyed, and dazed and amazed
we found ourselves alone. It was now near sunset
and we made our way back to Natéte in a very unhappy frame of mind. When we reached our house,
the three of us held a council as to what we should do.
Should we try and make for the Nyanza, and get on
board our boat? Should we quietly wait the coming
of Mujasi to carry out our sentence in the morning?
We knew well that he would use his power with the
utmost rigour, and our final decision was to send up a

a large amount of cloth and try to propitiate the authorities. So we made up six loads, which we sent to the king, and six more to the Katikiro, and in great suspense we awaited the result. Soon our messengers came back bringing the cloth. Is our gift then refused? No, it is only that it is late, and the king will receive it to-morrow. The Katikiro graciously accepts his bales, and sends back to say we are his brothers. When Mackay and I reached our quarters, the first thing we did was to warn all our adherents and all who were staying at the Mission to take flight. But, one young fellow, named Seruwanga, would not go. Like Lot, he lingered. I went out and asked him what madness it was that possessed him and made him loiter when there was such danger. His kindly reply was, "I'm going, my friend." A little later I again went out, and there he was; I became angry, and bade him leave at once, and he left, but alas, too late, and that evening he was seized. Mukasa Samweli, of whom I have spoken, hearing of our trouble, came down late at night under cover of darkness to show his friendship. Edward, another Mukasa, one of the first who accepted Christianity, also came to offer his sympathy. He was now keeper of Mutesa's mosque, a house which was built for the worship of Allah, and to the honour of his prophet, but which was always used as a Christian school. Afterwards Edward was made a powerful chief, but he met with a violent end, the fate of many of the actors in the scenes which I

am relating. The next day, Mr. O'Flaherty went up
to see the king and Katikiro, but met only with disappointment and failure. Mujasi came down with him,
and the insolent chancellor had the effrontery to appoint
Mr. O'Flaherty to search our house for Christians, the
Katikiro supplying him with his own myrmidons to aid
in the quest.

When no one was found, Mujasi returned, and soon
afterwards Sambo, Mackay's boy, was set free, but
Lugalama, Balibanange, and Bikutula, the others who
had been seized the previous day, were still in custody.
That afternoon Sambo came and told us terrible tidings,
that he had heard Mujasi was going to burn the boys
to death. This sad news grieved me to the very soul,
and I went out and sought some place to be alone.
After a while a sub-chief appeared with Bikutula.
I gave him a reward, and promised that if they
brought Lugalama back we would pay the price
of five slaves and redeem the others as well. Later,
they brought Balibanange. There remained only
Kakumba and Lugulama and Seruwanga, but these
were doomed; their only crime was that they had been
living with us. Lugalama was really condemned
because his master had given him to us and not to the
king or Katikiro.

When the messenger saw how eager I was to redeem
Lugalama he suggested that, if I gave him a larger
present, the child's safety would be ensured; so I gave
him some of the fine gold thread of great value, used

for embroidery, and promised him more when he came
with Lugalama ; and, though he must have known all
the time that the lads were dead, he accepted the bribe,
and appeared to undertake our errand. I made no
attempt to go to the authorities myself, as I knew that
my doing so would only irritate them and make the
murders more certain than ever, while in my heart I
could hardly believe that they would actually take
place. Lugalama and Kakumba, when first arrested,
were taken into a house, and Kakumba was beaten
in accordance with a common Buganda custom in the
treatment of prisoners. They had compassion on
Lugalama and gave him some food. Next day they
were taken to the king's enclosure and their sentence
was pronounced, Mujasi being the chief accuser.
Sebwato, Lugalama's former master, tried to save him
but in vain.

And so the three boys, Seruwanga, Kakumba, and
Lugalama, were led away to death, a mocking crowd
following them. "Oh, you know Isa .Masiya (Jesus
Christ)," said Mujasi. "You know how to read."
"You believe you will rise from the dead ? Well, I
shall burn you and see if it be so." These were some
of the mocking taunts which they endured, and loud
was the laughter which greeted such sallies. But the
young Christians, as some reported, answered boldly
and faithfully. Seruwanga was a daring fellow, and I
can well believe that when Mujasi mocked he would
sing, "Killa Siku tuusifu" ("Daily, daily sing the

praises "), as all were reported to have done. Kakumba
too had come to us when all others were afraid, and
perhaps his voice joined in the song. But what could
have been in poor little Lugalama's heart but the
haunting, over-mastering horror of death—and such a
death! What a *via dolorosa* was that which these
doomed captives were now to tread! But there were
none who dared to beat upon their breasts and show
the sorrow that they felt, though there were many
sympathising friends who followed, many compassionate hearts that God had touched with a pity which
perhaps before they had never known. One of these
was Kidza, Mujasi's "musali" or guide, and it was
from him, gentle, loving, and brave, one of God's
noblest martyrs, that I heard this story.

He told me how the mob, carrying gourds of banana-
cider, wound on their way till they reached the borders
of a dismal swamp called Mayanja, a place I had often
visited with Lugalama. Here they halted. Part of
the crowd bring firewood, others make a kind of rough
framework, under which the fuel is heaped. Then the
prisoners are seized, and a scene of sickening cruelty
is enacted. Some lay hold of Seruwanga, others of
Kakumba, and others of Lugalama, brandishing their
long curved knives. Seruwanga has committed his
cause to Him who judgeth righteously, and the cruel
knife cannot wring from him a cry ; bleeding he is cast
into the fire. Kakumba appealed to Mujasi Mujasi
believes in Allah the All-Merciful—he pleaded a

relationship with him; but, alas! there is as much mercy in the knife in the executioner's hand as in Mujasi's heart, and he too undergoes the short agony and the flame.

And now the saddest scene of all. Mujasi bids them treat Lugalama as they treated the others. Surely even these men, hardened by frequent executions, have never had to do a deed like this. They come nearer and he cries out, "Oh, do not cut off my arms; I will not struggle—I will not fight! Only throw me into the fire!" Surely this was the saddest prayer ever prayed on this sad earth—"Only throw me into the fire!" How like young Arthur pleading for his eyes!

> "Alas! what need you be so boisterous rough?
> I will not struggle—I will stand stone-still,
> .   .   .   .   .
> And I will sit as quiet as a lamb.
> I will not stir, nor wince, nor speak a word."

The butchers do their work and mar what was so wonderfully made, and the poor bleeding boy is placed on the framework that the slow fire may finish what the cruel knife has begun. A wail of anguish goes up, becoming fainter and fainter—a last sob, and then silence.

Musali stood sadly watching the sorrowful scene, wondering perhaps whether his turn may be next, when Mujasi, drunken with blood, came to him. "Ah, you are here! I will burn you too and your household. I know you are a follower of Isa (Jesus)." "Yes, I am," said Musali, "and I am not ashamed of it!" Never a truer word was said, and never a braver man spoke. Mujasi then left him.

What shall I say of that day of waiting, hoping, praying, fearing—praying not vainly, though at the very time the awful deed was being perpetrated ?

> "O mother! praying God will save
> Thy sailor. While thy head is bowed
> His heavy-shotted hammock-shroud
> Drops in its vast and wandering grave."

Such prayers are not vain as they may seem, but the answer to them is yet to come. That was a day when the wrongs of Africa came home to me and burnt themselves deep into my very soul—that day when Lugalama fell asleep, January 31st, 1885.

HE FELL ASLEEP.

> He fell asleep. No troubled dreams oppress him,
> He moaneth not; lying in Jesus' breast,
> No terrors of the darkness now possess him;
> He lieth in the light at perfect rest.
>
> Sometimes he lay so still that I would listen
> With a strange awe, and half suppose him dead ;
> And at the thought my eyes with tears would glisten
> As I stood o'er this loved child's little bed.
>
> O God of Love! Thy Love no shadow knoweth,
> No evil cloud of darkness o'er it lowers,
> No bitter blast of coldness o'er it bloweth—
> Forgive the sin of love so weak as ours.
>
> And yet our love, tho' by corruption clouded,
> Is still a spark of flame that fell from Thee,
> Which yet shall shine, no more by shadows shrouded,
> In Thy great light, O God, eternally.

CHAPTER XIV.

The Arabs sent down a message of sympathy with us in our trouble, and Hamisi and Ali bin Sultan came themselves to see us the following day. Ali bin Sultan afterwards showed us the bitterest hostility, but at this time the Arabs all visited us, and, whatever their real feeling may have been, nothing could have been kinder than the way in which they acted towards us.

A few days later Mwanga sent for Mackay, and when Mackay spoke of the murder of the boys, declared that he knew nothing about it, and said that the chief judge and Mujasi were only peasants, while he himself alone was king. This denial on his part was untrue, for the outrage was committed, if not at his instance, at any rate with his connivance. During these dark days the many faithful friends whom we reckoned among the native Christians still continued their visits. Among these were Samweli, most faithful of all, Sebwato, Gabunga the young admiral, and several others. They came usually at night, for our house was guarded all day; but in less than a fortnight this terrible storm had blown over. The Katikiro sent down to remove the guards who were watching our house, and permission was given to all who wished to bring us food for sale and to come for medicine. This was practically granting us permission to teach.

In spite of these favourable signs it was quite clear to us that our position was very precarious and uncertain, and so we determined to try and get as much printing done as possible. Mackay, with great foresight, had, on first coming to Africa, brought out a printing press with him. During the eight years which had elapsed it had passed through various adventures, and parts of it had been damaged and destroyed in a fire at the mission. Mackay, however, now made the missing pieces and put the whole together, and we were able to make printing our principal occupation ; and it was well that we took this opportunity, for the cruel outrages which I have described in the last chapter, so far from deterring others from coming to us to be taught, bore immediate fruit in largely-increased numbers of learners, and redoubled the interest felt in our work. We printed hundreds of reading-sheets and spelling-sheets, which were eagerly bought, and we began to put into type the Gospel of St. Matthew. From morning till night, eager and intelligent readers surrounded us. Mukasa was a constant visitor. He said to me one day, "Do not call me Mukasa—Mukasa is dead. I am Samweli." This boy went home and taught his mother, who idolised him, and then the two together taught his old grandmother. He also taught his half-brother Engiri (peccary), and Ali Wali, a very nice little boy, who was

afterwards accidentally burned to death in one of the
fires which are so frequent and so fatal in Buganda.
The whole family, in spite of the displeasure and
vexation of their relations, decided to throw aside all
their ancestral relics and charms, for their new religion
did not allow them any longer to consider sacred the
animal which represented their kyika or clan, the
explanation of which I have already given.

Mwanga's sisters, too, were eager readers; but
whether they reformed their evil way of living I much
doubt. One of them, named Mwafu, who chose the
name of Eve when baptised, was very unassuming and
modest—she was duly married with Christian rites; but
the queen-sister, though clever and intelligent, scanda-
lised the Church by her lack of chastity, for which she
was degraded from her high position by Mwanga's order.
Another princess also brought disgrace upon the Church
by the same scandalous behaviour. She finally was
won over to his faith by her Roman Catholic lover;
yet, in spite of her weakness, she proved herself our true
friend, and on one occasion, as will be seen hereafter,
saved the mission by a timely warning and practical
advice which we found of great value.

Mwanga for the present showed us no increased
hostility, and bad as he was, we yet felt that his
deposition would mean the utter ruin of the mission,
a belief which was fully borne out by the events which
subsequently took place in Buganda. Rumours that
Mwanga's position was uncertain now began to multiply,

and reports that his deposition was imminent reached us continually. Earnest and thoughtful men were at this time coming to us in large numbers, and not a few were baptised.

One of the old king's counsellors, Engobya, the father of a large number of most earnest readers, advised that we should be killed, for the chiefs with some show of reason looked with the gravest suspicion upon the new teaching, which they said induced "Kyeju," insolence. And no wonder that the philosophy which opens the eyes to see the substance of things, and which sets up a glass wherein all things are reflected in a strange form, filled them with supreme fears. A teaching which put great for what they believed small, and noble for what they thought mean ; which, lacking the heroic aspects of Islam, could yet make men calmly appeal to a spiritual power and brave without excitement the direst death, was a puzzle to the rulers of the country ; and there need be no surprise that the new superstition appeared to be a height of Kyeju hitherto unattained in Buganda.

The next news which we heard was of the disgrace and banishment of Mukwenda, Earl of Singo, the chief agent in the plot to depose Mwanga ; and the day following some sixteen of the principal chiefs were driven from power. The rebellion was thus nipped in the bud by the sagacity and foresight of the astute chancellor, and his wayward and wilful puppet was still kept on the throne.

The chancellor or Katikiro was all along a believer in the old gods of his country. He had all the subtility of Arabs ; he adopted their dress, learned their language, outdid them in the suavity of manner and politeness which characterises them ; but in his heart he hated them as he hated us for being foreigners, and for their religion. I remember at one of my last interviews with him, he sent for his Christian books, and read a little. He had learnt his letters at the time when Christian reading was so much the fashion in Mutesa's day, but he and many other chiefs still clung to their old belief in Lubarè.

When the rebellion was crushed the king began to talk of sending some of his pages to England, and apropos of this asked why we never went to see him. A few days afterwards we heard that he had given orders to rob our cattle, which had the desired effect of causing us to decide to attend his " baraza," levee. I had determined never to see his face again if I could help it. So Mackay went up to the enclosure, and had a satisfactory interview with both king and chancellor. Not long after this, Mwanga sent a messenger with compliments and a couple of cows ; and the day following he sent another cow— ample compensation no doubt in his blind eyes for the murder of our boys. Mackay again went to see him, and the king said that he would never part with the English, and directed him to write and invite the French priests to return to Buganda. To which of course Mackay agreed. Not long after this, the king again sent a couple of cows, with the request that we should go and see him.

Towards the end of April of 1885, news reached us that Emin Pasha was making his way to the coast with five ranks (regiments) of soldiers. This information came from Sembuzi, who may be remembered as the officer who deserted Stanley. A few days later, we heard that Emin and another European (Capt. Casati) were at Mruli with only thirty men. On the 3rd of May, in the afternoon, a rumour reached us that the Katikiro had given orders that the people who came to us to learn should be seized. But the next day Mackay had a favourable interview with him, and heard that Emin Pasha had been refused leave to pass by Kabarega. The Katikiro promised he would send an armed force to relieve him.

One of the pages came one day in great glee, this was Mwanga (Silas), to tell how a priest of Lubarè (of the old religion) had been beaten by the king's orders. I pointed out to this young enthusiast that persecution was wrong, and that what happened to the followers of Lubarè to-day might happen to the followers of Isa (Jesus) to-morrow.

About the middle of May, Mackay went to Musalala in the boat. While he was away, Mwanga sent for me. One of his favourite pages came out to meet me when I arrived at the king's enclosure to ask if I could mend a clock. I sent back to say I was a teacher and not a clock-maker. Mwanga desired to ignore this, being misled by the representations of those who were hostile

to our creed, but it was a point we always wished to
maintain. The king held that the privilege of living in
Buganda at the court of so great a monarch as himself
was quite reason enough for our remaining in the country
without teaching our religion; our contention was that
we only consented to stay in order to teach.

Had I known, however, that the clock only wanted
winding up, I should gladly have done that for him.
Kato, the page who took my message, " re-delivered " me
in a very polite manner. He was one of the Frenchman's pupils, and a great friend of mine, as was also
Nyonyi Entono. These lads frequently sent presents
of goats as a token of their kindly feeling. The king
simply said " Very well." I waited all day for an
audience, which was not vouchsafed. This was the first
time for six months that I had been up to the king.

About this time, June of 1885, there was another
rumour abroad that the Christians were to be seized;
and on Sunday the large numbers who attended church
quietly dispersed. The Arabs' slaves and our Mahometan coast men (servants) had a fight the same afternoon, and the Arabs went up to the king to lodge a
complaint against us. The king sent down to say we
were to come and plead the case against the Arabs.
We sent back to say that our servants and the Arabs
were all Wangwana, coast people, and that we had no
quarrel with the Arabs—let them settle it between themselves. So our men went and pleaded, and gained the
case. That day Mackay arrived from Musalala in the

boat, bringing the news of Gordon's death and the fall of Khartoum. The fight between our servants and the Arabs' slaves of a few days ago now broke out again, and many heads were broken on each side, and the captain of our boat badly speared.

On this occasion Mackay went and complained to the authorities, and judgment was again given against the Arabs. The chief ground of the quarrel probably was that our Zanzibar men were in the pay of Christians; though the immediate cause was some dispute at the market which was held just above our house, on an open space, where you could buy beef and vegetables, cloth or slaves—anything, in fact, from a Muhuma girl to a bundle of faggots.

Mackay took up a present to Mwanga as was customary on the arrival of the boat. He suggested to me that I should go and see the king. I told him how much I loathed the thought of looking upon this miserable murderer; to which he replied that it was no pleasure to him, but that he looked upon it as a needful duty. To this there was no replying, so I armed myself with a musical album—a present from some Liverpool sailor-boys—which Mwanga had seen and consequently coveted, and which I had refused to give him. Having gulped down my feelings, I went one morning; and though I was not admitted to the royal presence, my gift was accepted. I waited patiently the whole day, and the conditions for waiting were not unpleasant. The place we used as a waiting-room was the royal store-house;

and the king's store-keepers were nearly all Christians, and were most polite and kind. Little pages, Kibebefu, Mwanga, Kago, and others, were lying about on the floor of the house learning their A B C. During these times of waiting I made the acquaintance of Kiwewa, eldest son of Mutesa and elder brother of Mwanga, who has been made king in the recent changes. I met also Mwanga's two younger brothers, who were at large, one of whom, Kayondo, was also afterwards chosen to be king, though he does not appear to have actually reigned. That day Mwanga did not grant me an audience, and the three following days I went up to the enclosure, but did not see the king. I met, however, Alexandro, one of our converts, who held the chieftainship of Namfumbambi, of which I have spoken elsewhere. He told me that he had been accused of being a Christian, and that he had been beaten by the Katikiro's orders and driven out of his chieftainship.

Alexandro was soon given another office. He was of noble blood, and was never long without some post in the king's service. He, like the majority of those of whom I speak, was in another year to meet with a bloody death for his faith.

Another Christian chief, Mulya gonja ("eater of the sweet plaintain"), was at this time lording it over all the chiefs in the country, having been appointed to "kuba" the "kibuga" (set up the king's enclosure). He had the right to command the services of all the king's vassals in the making of the royal enclosure; and to seize and imprison delinquents. He was of a very proud and overbearing nature, and rigorously put in force his authority. We feared much for him, as he was naturally most unpopular. He was the Edward who visited us in our first great trouble, and was one of Mackay's earliest pupils, and among the first five baptized in Buganda. He was afterwards killed by another chief, for which Mwanga caused his slayer to be hewn in pieces.

The fourth time I visited Mwanga my perseverance was rewarded by an audience. After keeping me waiting the whole day, he sent for me. There were only a few boys with the king, and an elderly woman, probably some lady of distinction. Nyonyi Entono, and Kagwa, now young men, were sitting in the door-way. When I entered the house, Mwanga bade me be seated. I had brought him a hat with which he was much pleased. After some talk about the hat, he said, "Has Mackay gone to the Nyanza?" I replied that he had. Then he said, "Can you swim?" I replied, "Yes, a little." He then asked about Gordoom (General Gordon) and Abdul Emin (Emin Pasha). He also asked about Baker, whose name he knew, as there were some wonderful stories afloat in Buganda as to Baker's prowess. He then asked about Bishop Hannington, and Godoli, the missionary Gordon and Wise, and the trader Stokes, and also about the French priests. This conversation was interspersed at intervals with the two first questions, "Has Mackay gone to the

Nyanza?" and, "Can you swim?" He then asked me
if I could dive. To which I replied that I could a little.
He kept remarking to his boys in a sort of aside, "He
is an Englishman," and, "Mackay is an Englishman,"
"Makai ali Mungereza." He said that I was "Mulungi,"
to which all agreed. So I said to him, "You are king,
and we must all bow to what you say, so you should
always say what is good and right." He agreed to
this; then he said, "Is the bishop an Englishman?" I
said, "Yes; but that we teachers did not reckon our,
selves of any country, but only people of 'Katonda,'
God." He then asked about the death of Gordoom
(General Gordon) and about the Mahdi. Then he said,
"If I go and fight with Nakaranga, will you come with
me?" I told him I thought it wrong to go on an
expedition to fight; if the enemy came here, it would
be a different matter. "If the Madhi comes here," I said
"and you fight him, I will help you." But I said, "I
thought the Madhi would eat us all up, that he had
many guns and cannons." He then remarked my
beard and my hair, and asked me if I could do a high
jump. I told him that I was getting too old to jump,
at which he laughed, and said, "Why, you're only a
youth! I am also a youth," he added. But I said, as
I had said to Roma, "Have I not a beard, has a youth a
beard?" He pointed to a few hairs on his own chin, and
said, "Have not I a beard, and yet I am a youth?"
"You," I said, "are a man." He then asked where
the Frenchmen were. To which I replied, that they

were on the Nyanza. Then he finished off by again asking if I could swim; a point as to which he seemed very curious. He wanted to know whether I could make cloth. At this time Mackay was making a loom, and a most marvellous spinning-jenny which worked admirably. He was attempting to make cloth out of plantain-fibre; but before he had time to give the machinery a fair trial, the storm of persecution and trouble broke upon us, and prevented its being continuously worked. After this long conversation, the king sent for a fat goat, which he presented to me. And I took my leave.

Mackay had been down to the lake and got the boat ready to receive the king, who had expressed a wish to go on board. However, the priests of Lubare would not allow the king to go on the lake, as they said that Mukasa, the Neptune of the Nyanza, had not yet been propitiated. Soon after this the French priests arrived, Pères Lourdel and Jeraud, together with a lay brother. We were always on very good terms with them, and I think by that time we all recognised that there was room for both parties, and that they had learnt the lesson that however much they objected to our doctrine, public denunciation of it was of no earthly use. Their former attacks had been made with an honest purpose, of frustrating what they held to be a dangerous and deluding heresy. But now there was nothing of the kind, and all our dealings with them were of the pleasantest description. I was at the king's enclosure

when the priests arrived ; they were called in by themselves and were well received, and Mwanga promised
to build them a house.

After they had gone I was summoned, and after some
not very interesting conversation, the king reverted to
the topic of swimming, "Can you swim?" "Yes, a
little." He sent for a fat goat and gave it to me.
Then he said, "Will you swim for me?" Swimming,
by the way, is a very rare accomplishment in Buganda.
Then he added, "Will you swim in my pond?" I
said, "I should be most happy." "When will you?"
said the king. "Whenever you wish," I answered.
"Will you come now?" he eagerly asked. "Is it not
too late," I replied. "You will not come now?" in
a disappointed tone. "Yes, now if you like." So up
got the king, stepped from his throne and took my
hand and led me out, followed by a crowd of pages.
and we made our way to the pond. It was rather
muddy, but I took off my clothes and gave them
to a bystanding boy to hold, and then I plunged in
and swam about to the king's great satisfaction
and delight. The king took my habiliments and
critically examined them. He pronounced them to
be "biyambalo birungi," beautiful garments, a praise
I was not so much pleased to hear, as the tailor who
made them might have been, for I feared the next
thing would be a polite request for them. The king,
however, was in high good humour and did not beg
for anything. He praised my patience for waiting so

long to see him ; and as I was going away I was warmly
congratulated for having swum and for having shown
the king that my saying I could swim was not a lie,
which I suppose he suspected.

In July of this year the Christians met and balloted
for certain elders or church council. We felt this to
be a very necessary step, for in case of our being sent
away, we wished them to have some organisation of
their own. These elders were authorised to conduct
service, and to preach in the absence of the missionaries. Shortly before this, my servant Tom had taken
his departure. He had been engaged for two years, but
waited with me several months over his time. I had
a little boy named Benjy, a Musoga, who used to sweep
my room. I had got so into the habit of leaving
everything with Tom and my Muhuma boy, Lugalama, that I allowed Benjy, a lad of about twelve or
thirteen, to have the run of the place. He began
a course of systematic robbery on a large scale,
and I discovered him at last, owing to the fact of
his stealing a needle. When I once suspected that
he was a thief, I began to look at my things, and
found he had rifled every place where he could lay
his hands. He had been induced by some men who
lived near to rob me. I gave him a thorough good
thrashing, and chained him up for nearly a month.
After that I trusted no more small boys for a time.
Towards the end of August of the year 1885, Mackay
was busy superintending the making of a rope for

M

the king's flag-staff. A Madagascar man, named Toli,
who was the King's "fundi," or carpenter, was to put
up the mast. He utterly failed, since he cut the good
rope which Mackay had made and then tried to join
it. The rope gave way, and the whole thing came
crashing down and killed one or two men.

Mackay had warned them that it would not do; but
they turned a deaf ear to him. The king was disappointed and vexed, and, we heard, abused us roundly.
After failing in rearing his mast, he suddenly gave out
that he was going to "Kutabala," literally raid; but
when carried out in his own country it was more of a
royal progress. He gave orders that Mackay and Père
Lourdel were to accompany him, the others were to
stay at home and keep the house. The chief Kibare
was the "Musigere" (*locum tenens*, or regent in the
absence of the king).

Mwanga, having already begun to kill people, appeared as if he could not stop. There seems to be a
frightful fascination in this passion for blood, which
fortunately is as uncommon as it is unspeakably
horrible. Accounts now came in of repeated butchery
committed by the orders of the rapidly deteriorating
tyrant. And rumours of discontent with the king
were rife—one chief reason being "teyazala abaana"
("he had no children").

At the beginning of September our letters arrived, but
the news which they brought and what came of it I
must relate in the next chapter.

CHAPTER XV.

THE letters which we received brought us definite news of the German occupation of Usagára, and the startling intelligence that Hannington, now Bishop of East Equatorial Africa, intended to make his way to Buganda, following Thomson's route through the Masai country.

It was clear that the Bishop could not have received our letters warning him that he should exercise caution, and telling him about the late outrage, one of the reasons of which the Katikiro had said was that we were hiding white men at Buvuma to the east. However, there was one reassuring point in the Bishop's letter; he announced his intention of proceeding to Kavirondo, south of the jealously guarded territory of Busoga, and ordered that the mission boat should meet him there in October. A Mahometan Belooch had obtained a passage in our boat, and knew all the coast news, so that Mackay and I thought it would be better to tell Mwanga about the German occupation, and the Bishop's coming to Kavirondo, before the Belooch had time to do so. The Bishop had been assured that the Germans would thwart our missions in every way, and had therefore determined

M 2

to find another road to the lake rather than pass through
territory occupied by Germany.

It is, however, only just to the Germans, who occupied
the East African stations, to say that they have always
treated English missionaries with respect and courtesy
and have even gone out of their way to show us kindness.

On the 25th of September, 1885, Mackay and I took
Mwanga a present, and were granted an audience. We
told him our two important items of news—of the
German occupation and the Bishop's coming, which
made him and his counsellors appear somewhat per-
turbed. The king asked if other white men would
come with the Bishop. We thought that probably two
or three might be coming, so we could only reply that
we did not know ; but that he was an important person
and not likely to travel alone.

"Will the Askofu (Bishop) come to Busoga ?" asked
Mwanga. We thought we were fortunate in being able
to reply at once in the negative, and to assure the king
that he would only come to Kavirondo, pretty far to
the south. It will be seen, however, that the Bishop's
change of plan made our statements appear like
deliberate lying. We then told Mwanga that Ismail
the Belooch had news, and the king sent for him.

October, 1885.—The next day, Saturday, the king
summoned a great council of chiefs to discuss the whole
matter of the coming of the Bishop, and Sematimba, the
king's messenger, was called and instructed to go and
meet the Bishop, and report upon him, but not to bring
him.

I think, since the subject is one of deep interest, that it will be well to subjoin Mackay's very graphic account of the whole affair, which he sent home to the Church Missionary Society. After giving a description of Mwanga's character, and telling something of the work, he goes on :—

" Only a week ago I returned from a tour with the king and army through the west of his dominions. We were away twenty-six days in all. Père Lourdel also accompanied the expedition. We went by water from Busabala (Stanley's Usavara) to Ntebe, thence through Busi and Bunjako to the mouth of the Katonga. From there we struck north to Kyango and Nkanaga. At that place we halted some twelve days, a great review of the troops of Singo and Bulemezi being held. After that we returned N.E. and E. back to the capital. The route by water was the more pleasant, but that by land, though wearisome, the more interesting, as I was enabled to see the country as I had never seen it before. There was much of interest to record, and if I can find time to make a sketch and write out my notes of the tour, I shall do so for the sake of your geographical friends.

" On the road the king gave me several goats, and after returning he presented us with five head of cattle. There was no pillaging or robbery on the way. Much else, however, took place; more than enough to make one think with horror of what another such journey might be productive of.

" While we were still at Nkanaga, our mail arrived

here by the *Eleanor*. The brethren forwarded the letters
to me overland. I read with alarm of the German
doings at the coast, as we had telegrams to 17th June
mentioning that the German fleet had been ordered to
Zanzibar, while Lourdel had information that a force of
700 men was to occupy Usagára. Stokes had sent on
(giving him a free passage) a Belooch trader in the boat.
I meant to tell the king and Katikiro at once the news,
before the Belooch would have the opportunity, as were
he to tell his story first we would be suspected of being
implicated in the German designs, seeing we kept the
matter secret. I was, however, anxious to find out first
how much the Belooch really knew. I pumped some
of our men who had seen him, and from them I found
that the Germans had demanded from Seyed Burgash
the port of Bagamoyo, meaning to purchase it, but that
the Sultan had refused : hence they meant to fight him.
Further, that the Arabs of Unyanyembe were ordered
to return to the coast. Lourdel and I talked over the
matter and agreed to defer making the matter public
until our return to the capital. The matter was besides
much complicated by the letters from Bishop Hannington informing us of his intention to cross the Masai
country and strike the Lake at Kwa Sundu near Busoga.

"It is only natural that these natives be very jealous
for their land. In Buganda they look on the Lake as a
natural barrier, preventing invasion from the south.
When the Egyptians were north at Mruli, Mutesa was
ever trembling. From the west they fear nothing.

The Congo State may some day alarm them not a little. But the sore point is Busoga. From there they know the solid ground stretches off east all the way to the coast, and an army coming in that direction would find an open road. Mutesa used to twit me by saying: ' You white men would like much, would you not, to see the country behind Busoga ? That I would never allow.'

"I could see well how much our deep troubles this last spring owed their origin to the rumour of Thomson's visit to Busoga, although he was home again before they hardly knew here. What would it be now when the report came out that a great man was coming with a large party that very way to Buganda, while, at the same time, the white men were making war on Seyed Burgash ? The case looked serious. For it must be remembered that Baganda have no acquaintance with the geography of Europe, and look on all pale faces as of one race. All are called Bazungu. The Arabs have ever averred that we are only the pioneers of annexation—spies in fact. When Lieutenant Smith came here, Hamadi bin Ibrahim advised Mutesa to kill him and Wilson, as, he said, 'wherever these English put their foot, the land becomes theirs in time.' From that day onwards Mutesa was ever suspicious, yet prudent. When the Arabs continually reiterated their warnings as to our ultimately eating the country, Mutesa replied, 'Let the Bazungu alone. If they mean to eat the country, surely they will not begin at the interior.

When I see them begin to eat the coast, then I shall believe your words to be true.'

"Now, the beginning has been made at the coast—Bismarck *versus* Burgash. Who will win? And then, too, the English are coming to the jealously guarded land of Busoga, at the other side of Buvuma. One white man is supposed to be a host in himself.

"On Friday (25th inst.) Ashe and myself went to court to congratulate the king on his safe return, taking with us a box of sundry small articles as a present, it being our custom to give both him and the Katikiro something every time the boat brings us goods. His majesty expressed himself well pleased with the gift. We then told him that we wished his permission to let the boat go to Kavirondo to fetch his guest whom we had been expecting for some time. He was our Bishop, a chief of the Church, and our superior. We mentioned that his reason for coming that way was to avoid the Germans (Badutchi), who had some misunderstanding with Seyed Burgash. We did all we could to remove from the king's mind suspicion as to our having any connection with the Germans. We were cross-questioned as to the German's quarrel with the Sultan, and as to what they wanted there at all. Our information being very meagre, it was difficult for us to say much definitely, only we told simply what we heard, viz. that they had acquired a piece of territory, with the consent of the native chiefs, inland from Bagamoyo, that they had no designs against Burgash or his territory, but that the Sultan was provoking them by planting his flag in hosts of places where he had never done so before; and then they wished to purchase a port which Burgash refused to sell. 'Will Burgash fight?' asked the king. Answer: 'You are a king, and can best decide such a matter.' King: 'I believe he will come to terms with them without fighting.' Answer: 'We think you have judged rightly.' Kibare was present. He was regent at the capital in the king's recent absence. Kibare suggested that Burgash would fight. King: 'What are these Baduchi? Are they Bazungu?' Answer: 'Yes, they are Bazungu; a very powerful nation. They fought the French not long ago, and beat them, even capturing their king.' 'Which is the stronger, the English or the Germans?' 'The Germans are the stronger, especially by land. The English could not beat them if they went to war.' 'Ah,' said Kibare, 'if the English could not beat them, Burgash need not try.' King: 'Is the Bishop an Englishman?' 'Yes.' 'Is he bringing much bintu (goods)?' 'He will not come empty-handed, but he is a chief not of this world's goods, but of religion; he is a great teacher.' 'Do you want to go to fetch him?' 'I do not want to go myself, but we should like the boat to go to Musalala, where Mr. Stokes will join her and go to Kavirondo to try and find the Bishop.' 'Where is the Bishop just now?' 'He is probably at Chagga.' 'Is he coming through Busoga?' 'No, he means to reach the Lake somewhere in Kavirondo, leaving Busoga far to the north, and Ukerewe to the south.' ' Is he coming alone ? ' ' Not likely; he is a great man, and does not travel alone; he will have one assistant (chaplain ?) with him, and perhaps another.' 'Is Stokes coming with him ?' 'Perhaps; I don't know.' I then asked if he would kindly send a "mubaka" (messenger) with the boat, and to this he consented. He gave us a cow on leaving.

"Next morning the king had a council of his chiefs. Present—Kibare, Kangao, Mukwenda, Pokino, Mugema, Nsege, Ngobya, Kyimbugwe, and Kolugi—all important personages. The Katikiro was absent. Mwanga made a speech to them on his relations with white men from the beginning. When he came to the throne he wanted Bazungu, and had sent Sematimba with me to Musalala to bring three Englishmen. They refused to come. He therefore sent for the Frenchmen at Ukumbi. They came at once. He then narrated every word of our conversation with him yesterday, adding, what I have omitted to mention above, that we had asked him to build a house for the Bishop, as we were short of accommodation. The chiefs then expressed their opinions on the situation. All seemed to be of one mind, that white men were all one, and that we and the Bishop were only the fore-runners of war. We were only waiting for our head-men to come, when we would commence to eat the country. Kangao would go and fight the Bishop. Ngobya said that when you see running water you may expect more to follow; the only way was to stop it at the source. We were drawing these white men here : hence he counselled that we should be killed so as to stop the evil. It had been said that if white men were killed the country would be ruined. No such result had followed the murder of two white men in Ukerewe ; Lukonge was still there. Mugema remarked that our house had been a year and a half in building; who would undertake a like work again ? The general opinion was that the Bishop was not to be allowed to come, especially as he was coming by a *back door* through the Masai and Busoga. [N.B. —The Baganda call the Masai ' Basaba,' and know of their presence to the north-east of Busoga. They do not know that the tribe extends also southward, as far as the Wahumba.]

" The king suggested that Sematimba be sent in the boat, to inquire and spy how many men the Bishop had with him, and what goods, and return in the first instance to report. Kolugi's advice was that the whole party proceed first to Musalala, instead of establishing themselves over there, behind Buvuma; and that the king might send there for them, if he liked. Kangao remarked that seven ships of Bazungu had been lost off the coast of Buvuma, as the Lubarè (Lake spirit) would not allow them to come here.

"Kolugi's advice was adopted, and Sematimba received instructions accordingly not to bring the Bishop's party direct here, but to convey them to Musalala, and return here to report.

"Next day was Sunday, and we had our hands full with classes and services all day. On Monday we meant to go again to court and see the Katikiro, if possible, as well as the king, and explain again our absolute non-connection with the Germans, while we meant to assent to the proposal that the party go to Musalala first. Mr. O'Flaherty thought that it was necessary for him to go to meet the Bishop, and try, if possible, to bring him direct to Buganda. He accordingly went to court, and saw the Katikiro in his own place. That official expressed his alarm at the news he had heard, and closely cross-questioned O'Flaherty on what he knew. The king was afterwards seen, and after O'Flaherty's explaining by the aid of a map that the Bishop's route does not lie near Busoga, he obtained permission to go himself in the boat and bring the party straight on here, the king alleging that he wished to have many Bazungu, English, French, Germans, and all, at his court. The Arabs were present, and reported on the doings of the Belgians at Unyanyembe and Karema, and also in Manyuema (now in Congo State).

"Sematimba was not there, however; but he came to me afterwards, saying that he was perplexed, as the king had given him positive instructions to convey the Bishop and party to Musalala, while he had not been sent for to get other instructions to bring them direct to Buganda. He could not, therefore, go until he had seen the king again. I advised him to do so. He

waited at court all day yesterday, but did not see his
majesty. Meantime Mr. O'Flaherty has changed his
mind, and thinks he will not go.

" *Wednesday*, 30*th.*—Mr. O'Flaherty waited all day
at court, but did not see the king. In the evening we
together agreed that I should try to see the king next
morning and endeavour to get the messenger definitely
appointed.

" *Thursday, October* 1*st.*—Took with me a large
school-map of Europe; found a grand " burzah "; king
on throne; Katikiro and all great chiefs present; body-
guard drawn up, and lords of the cord predominating.
Evidently important business on hand. I felt very
thankful to have this opportunity of seeing king and
chiefs together. It was indeed providential.

" After salaams, unrolled map of Europe; said that
I had brought it to show that Bulaya (as they call
Europe) was not one country, but contained many
kingdoms, each having a different race, language, and
king; just as in Africa there were Baganda, Ban-
yamwezi, Bakedi, Bagogo. We were English, and were
in no way responsible for the doings of the Germans.
We had not brought them to Zanzibar, nor had we
anything whatever to do with them. We were accused
of wishing to ' eat ' the country, but in all these years
we had eaten nothing. We were only friends and
subjects of the king, and had no sinister motives.

" On this from all sides rose the cry, ' Who told you
that we said you meant to take our country ? ' ' Every-

body says so : besides, I can understand that you have reason for alarm.'

"The king, Katikiro, and Pokino (formerly Kyambalango) then spent some time in animated conversation, but in whispers. After which the Katikiro begged to assure me most positively that they had no suspicion of us, and that I had been misinformed (diplomatic truth !).

"I continued, that 'I had now been in the country more years than any other European; that my first request on arrival was for permission to bring Mr. Pearson and party. They had come and seen the king and had given presents to him and the Katikiro, and all had left without doing any harm. I had asked in like manner for canoes to be sent for Mr. Stokes, and Mr. O'Flaherty, and Mr. Ashe, one after the other; and these had all shown themselves to be men of peace.' Now I asked the king to send for our Bishop, who was an Englishman like ourselves; let him send a messenger in our boat and bring him. He was the king's guest.' The king at once replied, 'I have given you Sematimba, he will go.' On Sematimba being called forward, I asked again : 'This messenger will go in the boat and bring the Askofu (Bishop) and his brethren direct to this ?' Mugema said, 'No ; ' and others echoed, 'No.' Kolugi was sitting behind the Katikiro. He rose and came forward, and, kneeling in front of the throne, said, 'Sematimba will go to Musalala, where he will find Stokes, and go with him to find the Askofu, and take the

latter back to Musalala, where he (Bishop) must wait
until the king sends for him.'

" The Katikiro also added that Sematimba was to
remain with the Bishop at Musalala, and send on here
his assistant, Ensubuga, in the boat to report concerning
the new party and their goods. All assented to this
finding, which, by the way it was brought forward, was
evidently a previous resolution. The king also assented,
and so did I. I then explained that Mr. O'Flaherty
did not now mean to go, but that if the king wished
one of us to go in the boat, I was prepared to do so.
To this Mwanga replied, " I wish you to stay where
you are." Orders were given for a cargo of plantains to
be supplied, and Sematimba left. The court soon after
rose."

With reference to the route which Hannington now
followed, the Rev. E. C. Dawson, in his admirable
biography of the Bishop, is at some pains to defend the
choice of this Masai road. Of his eloquence there can
be no doubt; but in spite of his enthusiastic manner
of writing, he can hardly carry his more cautious
readers with him. Hannington, while he acted on the
advice and with the countenance of Sir John Kirk and
General Matthews, chose this road notwithstanding the
adverse opinion of the only traveller who had preceded
him—Mr. Joseph Thomson.

Mr. Dawson, too, is surely mistaken in the opinion
which he expresses of the ordinary caravan route

between Zanzibar and Unyanyembe. Only one missionary, as far as I am aware, has died from the effects of the journey on this route, and his death was due, I have been told, to the same cause which so nearly proved fatal to Bishop Hannington himself, want of proper necessaries.

Physical suffering, and fatigue, and fever are, I suppose, the natural accompaniment of travelling in a new country; but Thomson seems to have suffered more from these than the average traveller on the other route. I do not wish to minimise the difficulties of the road which I myself have travelled four times; but it is my deliberate opinion that for the present it is the more feasible and less dangerous route of the two under discussion, and I think as regards the healthiness there is not much to choose between them.

Hannington, as one of his reasons, mentions that Stokes' caravan had been attacked in Ugogo by robbers. But this was the Bishop's mistake. Robbers, properly speaking, only attack in the forests. In an inhabited district an attack of this kind could never be made, unless with the direct orders of the chief. It was a mistake which the Bishop made in Busoga, and was one of the causes which led to his death.

The occasion he refers to when mentioning the attack upon Stokes was when Stokes had given orders to his caravan to proceed before the "hongo" question had been finally settled.

In the account given of this in a missionary paper

Stokes' men are said to have fired in the air. Most of them did so ; but the writer did not know that it was for the same reason that so many warriors fire into the air, namely that they were too frightened and too nervous and too unskilful to fire anywhere else. Two of their bullets, however, going through the air, struck two Wagogo men by chance and killed them.

To return now to Buganda. The boat was sent off to look for the Bishop, and we settled down again to work. Readers flocked about us, and there were weekly meetings of the Native Church Council, at which various questions were discussed and decided.

And so a month passed away.

As a rule a journal is not interesting, but I think that in this particular instance what I wrote when in the middle of the trouble which was now to fall upon us will perhaps make the situation more clear, so I extract the following from my diary :—

1885. *Oct. 25th, Sunday.*—In the morning, Entanda (Gideoni), one of the court lads, brought the news of the arrival at Luba of two white men, who he says are Englishmen, one an elderly man, and the other a youth, and that they have twenty Wangwana (porters) with them. Later on, Sekajija Marko, a little page, came with the further news that the Englishmen were prisoners, and in the stocks. We were very much concerned, and Mackay and I, when we heard of our countrymen, strongly suspected that it must be Bishop Hannington and his chaplain. Still it might be some

N

other traveller, and we knew that the German explorer, Dr. Fischer, was leading an expedition to the Victoria Lake. It might be he. We called our Native Church Council together, and decided at once to dismiss the congregation, which had by this time assembled for service, and that Mackay and I should go up to the king's enclosure, and endeavour to see Mwanga.

Presently in came Yusufu Nasala, and told us that the king has decided to kill the prisoners, adding that one of them has lost a thumb. Immediately I heard that I said " It is the bishop." For this mark of identification could hardly be mistaken, as a gun-powder accident had deprived Hannington of his thumb in his early days. Mackay and I lost no time in making our way to the king's enclosure. As we entered the Wankaki (great gate) little Sekajija and another page who called himself Noah came up and whispered as we passed, " Bagenze kubatta " (They have gone to kill them). We entered and waited long in Kolugi's store. Kolugi is a person of considerable importance, and can muster some one or two thousand warriors. The king refused us an audience, and bade us tell Kolugi what we wanted. Both Kolugi and Pokino, who were present at the council which Mwanga held to decide upon murdering Bishop Hannington, at first professed entire ignorance of the whole affair. We said, " This is a matter which all Buganda knows; why are you deceiving us ? " We carefully detailed to Kolugi the news which we had heard, and besought him to carry our words to the king, and to ask him to grant us an interview. He went to the king, and presently returned, saying, " The Kabaka commands you to go to the chief judge. Our last pleading before the chancellor had been so unsatisfactory, that we refused, saying that we were the king's guests alone, and we added, " The Englishman in Busoga is our brother, and the king knows that we told him the Askofu (Bishop) was coming to see him. For what reason has he now sent to have him killed ? "

" The king knows nothing of these words," answered Kolugi. " Why do you persist in deceiving us ? " we said ; " you are our friend ? We have heard the names of the messengers despatched by the King—Wakoli * the gate-keeper and Musoke, the page ; the former to kill the Askofu, and the latter to count his " bintu " (things)—and we know that they have already gone."

Kolugi again went and stood before the king, and after some time, came out bringing Mwanga's reply. " The king commands you to come to-morrow, and he will give you his messenger to go and save them." " To-morrow," we replied, " will be too late. Oh, let him send now."

Kolugi offered to return once more ; but Mwanga had gone out of his inclosure by the back way, which led to his pond, and did not return till nightfall, when we had to go, since the great gates were closed. As

* Same name as one of the paramount chiefs of Busoga, from whom he must be distinguished. The other chief of Busoga, Luba, it was who captured Bishop Hannington.

our last earthly resource we offered Kolugi a large bribe
if he would send post haste and delay the messengers.
This he promised to do; but we had little confidence
either in his willingness or ability to do so. While
waiting, Samweli slipped a letter into my hand which
he had written. He was one of the assistant store-
keepers, and had heard the chiefs when they told us
of the ignorance of the king and themselves of our
bishop's danger. The letter ran thus:—

"Munange sebo (My friend, sir)—Believe not their
words—they have deceived you; most certainly the
messengers have gone to kill them."

" Samweli."

"In the courtyard of the storehouses there were
sitting some miserable captives taken from Busoga in
a late raid. I noticed them carefully to see whether
they got any food. It was a fasting day for us, so that
a fellow feeling made us sympathise with them; but
the livelong day passed by and not a morsel did they
get. Some of them were women with young children
in their arms. I asked one of the guards if those
prisoners would get any food, and the reply was that
they would receive some on the morrow."

The above was written at about 4 A.M. on Monday,
Oct. 26th, 1885. My diary of that miserable day ends
thus:—"Their death—if it be God's will—and ours,
which will also probably follow: O God, may it be a
step towards better things for this unhappy land! O
God, look upon it——"

CHAPTER XVI.

MEANWHILE, Hannington, knowing nothing of the state of things in Buganda, or of the suspicion caused by Thompson's coming, had made his way to Kavirondo, where the mission boat in charge of Mr. Stokes, of previous mention, had proceeded to look for him. Though Hannington himself soon left Kavirondo with fifty men, there still remained the bulk of his porters under the native pastor Jones; but, strange to say, Mr. Stokes heard no news of this caravan, and so he returned to Musalala.

As will be seen, the bishop's change of plan was most unfortunate, though under the circumstances it could hardly have been avoided.

Hannington, after leaving Kavirondo, journeyed north until he reached Busoga; and at Luba's, where he was stopped, he saw his first view of the Victoria Nile.

I give here his own account of his capture, and it will be seen how he mistook Luba's warriors, who were acting under the chief's orders, for robbers.

Strange to say, a few months later the journal came into our hands. Kulugi, the keeper of the king's stores, who had the custody of the things stolen from the bishop was, as I have said, to a certain extent our friend, and we had sent him a present of a small tusk of ivory, after which Mackay visited him and managed to obtain from him the bishop's writing-case, which contained the diary which he had been writing, it would seem, up to the hour of his death.

It was hardly a matter of wonder that my tears should fall as I read the familiar handwriting of the friend who had been a companion in months of weary travel and whom I had learned to know so well and to · respect so much.

If you can respect and love a man after living with him in Africa it means that in no small degree he has the highest qualities. This may seem a strange remark to make; but Africa proves a man, and he who issues unscathed from that furnace is pure gold indeed.

This is the journal of his few last days:—*

"*Oct.* 21*st*, *Wednesday.*—About half an hour only brought us to Luba's. The first demand was in a most insolent tone for ten guns and three barrels of powder; this, of course, I refused. They then demanded that I should stay three days; this I refused, and when the same demands were made, I jumped up and said, I go back the way I came.' Meantime the war drums beat. More than a thousand soldiers were

---

* I follow here mostly the editing of Rev. E. C. Dawson, the bishop's biographer, though my copy of the diary and his do not always agree.

assembled. My men implored me not to move, but
laughing at them I pushed them and the loads
through the crowd and turned back. Then came
an imploring message that I would stay but for a
short time. I refused to hear till several messages
had arrived; then, thinking things were turning my
way, I consented; said I would give a small present
and pass. My present was returned, and a demand
made that I would stay one day; to this I consented,
because I fancy this man can send me on in canoes
direct to Mwanga's capital, and save a week's march.
Presently seven guns were stolen from us; at this I
pretended to rejoice exceedingly, since I should demand
restoration not from these men, but from Mwanga. A
soldier was placed to guard me in my tent, and follow
me if I moved an inch. I climbed a neighbouring hill,
and, to my joy, saw a splendid view of the Nile, only
about *half an hour's distance,* country being beautiful ;
deep creeks of the lake visible to the south. I presently
asked leave to go to the Nile. This was denied me. I
afterwards asked my head man Brahim to come with
me to the point close at hand whence I had seen the
Nile, as our men had begun to doubt its existence ;
several * followed up, and one, pretending to show me
another view, led me further away, when suddenly
about twenty ruffians set upon us. They violently
threw me to the ground, and proceeded to strip me of
all valuables. Thinking they were robbers, I shouted

* "Several" here refers to Luba's people.

for help, when they forced me up and hurried me away, as I thought, to throw me down a precipice close at hand. I shouted again, in spite of one threatening to kill me with a club. Twice I nearly broke away from them, and then grew faint with struggling, and was dragged by the legs over the ground. I said, 'Lord, I put myself in Thy hands; I look to Thee alone.' Then another struggle and I got to my feet, and was thus dashed along. More than once I was violently brought into contact with banana trees, some trying in their haste to force me one way, others the other, and the exertion and struggling strained me in the most agonising manner. In spite of all, and feeling I was being dragged away to be murdered at a distance, I sang 'Safe in the arms of Jesus,' * and then laughed at the very agony of my situation—my clothes torn to pieces so that I was exposed; wet through with being dragged along the ground; strained in every limb, and for a whole hour expecting instant death; hurried along, dragged, pushed, at about five miles an hour, until we came to a hut into the court of which I was forced. Now, I thought, I am to be murdered. As they released one hand, I drew my finger across my throat, and understood them to say decidedly, 'No.' We then made out that I had been seized by order of the Sultan. Then arose a new agony. Were all my men murdered? Another two or three hours' awful suspense, during which time I was kept bound and shivering with cold, when, to my joy,

* My copy has the addition, "And, my God, I am Thine."

Pinto (the Goanese cook) and a boy were brought with
my bed and bedding, and I learnt that the Sultan had
seized me and simultaneously my men and loads, and
meant to keep me prisoner until he had received word
from Mwanga, which means, I fear, a week or more, nor
can I tell the exact truth of what they say. I am in
God's hands.

"*Oct.* 22*nd, Thursday.*—I found myself, perhaps
about ten o'clock last night, on my bed in a fair-sized
hut, but with no ventilation—a fire on the hearth, no
chimney for smoke; about twenty men all around me,
and rats and vermin *ad lib.*; fearfully shaken, strained
in every limb; great pain, and consumed with thirst.
I got little sleep that night. Pinto may cook my food,
and I have been allowed to have my Bible and writing
things also. I hear the men are in close confinement, but
safe, and the loads, except a few small things, intact.
Up to one o'clock I have received no news whatever, and
I fear at least a week in this black hole, in which I can
barely see to write. Floor covered with rotting banana
peel and leaves and lice; men relieving nature at night
on the floor; a smoking fire, at which my guards cook
and drink pombe; in a feverish district; fearfully
shaken, scarce power to hold up a small Bible. Shall I
live through it? My God, I am Thine.* Towards
evening I was allowed to sit outside for a little time,
and enjoyed the fresh air; but it made matters worse

---

* My copy here reads, "1 P.M., good broth, but no appetite to eat
it. However, if it was not here, I should no doubt feel starving."

when I went inside my prison again, and as I fell exhausted on my bed I burst into tears ; health seems to be quite giving way with the shock. I fear I am in a very caged-lion frame of mind, and yet so strained and shattered that it is with the utmost difficulty I can stand ; yet I ought to be praising His Holy Name, and I do.

" Not allowed a knife to eat my food with. The savages who guard me keep up an unceasing strain of raillery, or at least I fancy they do, about the Mzungu.

" *Oct. 23rd, Friday.*—I woke full of pain and weak, so that with the utmost difficulty I crawled outside and sat in a chair, and yet they guard every move as if I was a giant. My nerves, too, have received such a shock, that, hearing some loud yells and war cries outside the prison fence, I expected to be murdered, and simply turned over and said, ' Let the Lord do as He sees fit ; I shall not make the slightest resistance.' Seeing how bad I am, they have sent my tent for me to use in the daytime.* Going outside, I fell to the ground exhausted and was helped back in a gone condition to my bed. I don't see how I can stand all this, and yet I don't want to give in, but it almost seems as if Uganda itself was going to be forbidden ground to me.† The Lord only knows.

" *Afternoon.*—To my surprise my guards came kneel-

* My copy reads, " I implore to sleep here, but fear not. I said, ' Take away my boots, and how can I flee ? ' "

† In my copy, " Though I am far in the dominion, I have yet only looked upon the country itself."

ing down—so different from their usual treatment—and asked me to come out. I came out, and there was the chief and about a hundred of his wives come to feast their eyes on me in cruel curiosity.* I felt inclined to spring at his throat, but sat still and presently read to myself Matthew v. 44, 45, and felt refreshed. I asked how many more days he meant to keep me in prison. He said four more at least.† He agreed, upon my earnest request, to allow me to sleep in my own tent with two armed soldiers at each door. The object of his visit was to ask that I would say no bad things of him to Mwanga. What can I say good? I made no answer to the twice-repeated request. He then said if I would write a short letter and promise to say nothing bad he would send it at once. I immediately wrote a hasty scrawl (I scarce know what), but said I was a prisoner and asked Mackay to come. God grant it may reach; ‡ but I already feel better than I have done since my capture, though still very shattered.

" *Oct.* 24*th, Saturday.*—Thank God for a pleasant night in my own tent, in spite of a tremendous storm, and rain flowing in on the floor in streams. Personally I quite forgive this old man and his agents for my rough treatment, though even to-day I can only move with

* My copy has "cruel adversity," which makes sense.

† Here Mr. Dawson and I differ a good deal. May I venture to say that I cannot look on Mr. Dawson's changes as improvements. Hannington's own words, though often rugged, are always living pictures.

‡ This letter never came into our hands.

the greatest discomfort, and ache as though I had
rheumatic fever. I have, however, to consider the
question in another light : if the matter is passed over
unnoticed, it appears to me the safety of all white
travellers in these districts will be endangered, so I
shall leave the brethren, who know the country and are
most affected, to act as they think best. The day passed
very quietly. I amused myself with Bible and diary.

"*Oct. 25th, Sunday* (fourth day of imprisonment).—
Still a great deal of pain in my limbs. The fatigue of
dressing quite knocks me over. My guards, though at
times they stick to me like leeches, and, with two rifles
in hand, remain at night in my tent, are gradually
getting very careless. I have already seen opportunities
of escape had I wanted so to do, and I doubt not that in a
few days' time, especially if I could get a little extra
pombe brought to them, I could walk away quite easily,
but I have no such intention. I should be more inclined
to stop should they say ' Go,' to be a thorn in the old gentleman's side, and, I fear, from that feeling of contrari-
ness which is rather inborn. I send him affectionate
greetings and reports on my health by his messengers
twice a day. What I fear most now is the close confinement and utter want of exercise.

" When I was almost beginning to think of my time in
prison as getting short, the chief has sent men to
redouble the fence around me. What does it mean ? I
have shown no desire or intention of escaping. Has a
messenger arrived from Mwanga ? There is just time

for him to have sent word to tell them to hold me fast. The look of this has cast me down again.

" One of my guards, if I understand him rightly, is making me offers of escape. He has something very secret to communicate, and will not even take my boy into confidence. I do not, however, want to escape under the present circumstances ; but at the same time I take great amusement in watching and passing by various little opportunities. My guards and I are great friends, almost affectionate, and one speaks of me as ' My White man.' Three detachments of the chief's wives—they say he has one thousand nearly—have been to-day to see me. They are very quiet and well-behaved, but greatly amused at the prisoner. Mackay's name seems quite a household word. I constantly hear it.* My men are kept in close confinement, except two who come daily backwards and forwards to bring my food. This they take in turns, and implore, so I hear, for the job.

" *Oct.* 26*th, Monday* (fifth day in prison).—Limbs and bruises and stiffness better, but I am heavy and sleepy. Was not inclined to get up as usual, and, if I mistake not, signs of fever creep over me. Mackay should get my letter to-day, and sufficient time has passed for the chief to receive an answer to his first message sent before I was seized, the nature of which I know not, probably : ' White man is stopping here. Shall I send him on ? Waiting your majesty's pleasure.'

" If they do not guess who it is they will very likely,

* In my copy, " But of the others I scarce ever hear a word."

African fashion, talk about it two or three days first of
all, and then send a message back leisurely with
Mwanga's permission for me to advance.

"About thirty-three more of the chief's wives came
and disported themselves with gazing at the prisoner.
I was very poorly and utterly disinclined to pay any
attention to them, and said in English, ' Oh, ladies,
if you only knew how ill I feel, you would go.' When
my food arrived in the middle of the day I was unable
to eat—the first time, I think, since leaving the coast
I have refused a meal. To-day I am very broken-down
both in health and spirits, and some of the murmuring
feelings, which I thought had gone, have regained
hold upon me. Another party of wives coming, I
retired into the hut and declined to see them. A third
party came later on, and being a little better, I came
out and lay upon my bed. It is not pleasant to be
examined as a caged lion in the Zoo, and yet that is
exactly my state at the present time. My tent is
jammed in between the hut and high fence of the Boma,
so scarce a breath of air reaches me. Then, at night,
though the tent is a vast improvement on the hut, yet
two soldiers, reeking with pombe and other smells,
sleep beside me, and the other part of my guard, not
far short of twenty, laugh and drink and shout far into
the night, and begin again before daylight in the
morning, waking up from time to time to shout out to
my sentries to know if all is well. I fear all this is
telling on my health tremendously.

"*Oct. 27th, Tuesday* (sixth day as prisoner).—All I can hear in the way of news is that the chief has sent men to fight those parts we passed through. I begin to doubt if he has sent to Mwanga at all, but thinks I am in league with the fighting party, and is keeping me hostage. I begin the day better in health, though I had a most disturbed night. I am very low in spirits; it looks so, so dark, and have been told that the first messengers would return at the latest to-day. Last night the chief's messenger said perhaps they might be here as soon as Thursday, but seemed to doubt it. I don't know what to think, and would say from the heart, "Let the Lord do what seemeth Him good." If kept here another week I shall feel sure no messengers have been sent, and if possible shall endeavour to flee, in spite of all the property I must leave behind and the danger of the undertaking.

"Only a few ladies came to see the wild beast to-day. I felt so low and wretched that I retired within my den, whither they, some of them, followed me; but as it was too dark to see me, and I refused to speak, they soon left.

"The only news of to-day is that two white men, one tall and the other short, have arrived in Akola, and the Sultan has detained them. It is only a report that has followed me. I am the tall man, and Pinto, my Goa cook, the short one; he is almost always taken for a white man, and dresses as such. I fear, however, with these fearfully suspicious people, that it may affect me seriously. I am very low, and cry to God for release.

"*Oct.* 28*th, Wednesday* (seventh day's prison).—A terrible night; first with noisy drunken guard, and secondly with vermin, which have found out my tent and swarm. I don't think I got one sound hour's sleep, and woke with fever fast developing. Oh, Lord, do have mercy upon me, and release me. I am quite broken-down and brought low. Comforted by reading Psalm xxvii.

"In an hour or two fever developed very rapidly. My tent was so stifling that I was obliged to go inside the filthy hut, and soon was delirious.

"Evening; fever passed away. News comes that Mwanga has sent three soldiers, but what news they bring they will not yet let me know.

"Much comforted by Psalm xxviii.

"*Oct.* 29*th, Thursday* (eighth day's prison).—I can hear no news, but was held up by Psalm xxx., which came with great power. A hyena howled near me last night, smelling a sick man, but I hope it is not to have me yet."

His last night of weariness and pain had passed away, and little promise there seemed of morning joy, when suddenly Mwanga's messengers appeared, and coming in, they told him that the king of Buganda had sent for him. The previous night he had heard much beating of drums, as we had heard on the night preceding the day of Lugalama's death.

The messengers bade him come forth from his prison. He is pale and worn with fever; but very quiet now, very patient, but withal very noble; never so noble as now, never so ready to die as to-day. Quite broken-down and brought low, never had he reached so great a height. One of the messengers snatches up his Bible, another his portfolio, and another his sketch-book; and they lead him out, telling him he is soon to join his men.

There are, however, no signs of his men, and the way is long; another *Via dolorosa* is being passed. He is very weary, but he must not rest. There accompany him great numbers of Basoga warriors armed; these had been summoned by the war drums of the preceding night.

After two hours' walking the party reach an open space without the banana groves, where at last Hannington sees his men, not, as he expected, with their loads, nor carrying their guns and full of spirits at the thought of once more being on the road, but all bound, some with the " kaligo," heavy-forked branch, round their necks, stripped of their clothing, and many with their hands tied behind their backs. They now see their master led into the open where they are. He seems wonderfully calm, and turns as if to sit down—this is not allowed. A gun is fired, doubtless by Wakoli, and Hannington's guards begin to strip him of his clothing. He is quite passive in their hands. He has commended

o

his soul to Him who sits above kings. But the report* of his last words has come to us : "Tell the king," he said, "that I die for Buganda. I have bought this road with my life."

They had now forced him to his knees—fitting posture in which to die; so kneeling

> "And looking upward, full of grace,
> He prayed, and from a happy place
> God's glory smote him on the face."

Then the spears are plunged into that heart which had overflowed with such fervent love for his murderers and their race.

Such was the terrible scene which the bishop's followers had to witness, and we can partly enter into the feelings of sickening horror with which they saw the grim death inflicted on another which was immediately to be their own.

One of these men was destined to pass through this awful drama, and return to tell the thrilling tale. The warriors with a wild cry now sprang upon the defenceless porters, and soon the frightful butchery was accomplished; and then, as if half fearing what they had done, the army of the Basoga and Baganda murderers hurried away, leaving the dead lying where they had fallen. Night drew her curtain over the scene, and

---

* This was told us by friends who had many opportunities of seeing those who were actually present. Still, they are only given as a *report at second hand.*

when the moon came out she shone peacefully upon
the seeming sleepers ; alas,

> "The many men so beautiful,
> And they all dead did lie,"

and the long hours passed slowly away. Just before
dawn one of the sleepers moves ; seems to awake, sits
up, looks wildly round ; sinks back, remembers now
what it is, and these all about him are his dead companions. He has a ghastly wound, his bowels are
protruding through the gash ; again he painfully raises
himself, puts back his bowels, drags himself to where
he sees a banana leaf lying, puts it over the wound ;
and then, not staying to mark the faces of the dead,
with the dim instinct of preserving his life, he crawls
away. He cannot get far, he comes to a hut. He
is recognised ; but the simple folk who live there
have no sympathy with such deeds of blood as have
been enacted near them, and so they give this unhappy
fellow-creature food and shelter ; and, so a stranger in a
strange land, he meets with loving-kindness and hospitality until he is able to reach the Mission station at
the south of the lake.

CHAPTER XVII.

BAGANDA CONVERTS.

To return now to what was passing in Buganda. During these days we lived in constant expectation of being put to death. Reports of earnest conferences on the subject held by the king and chiefs daily reached us. We allowed all our boys to leave us and find refuge where they could. Hamisi, the Arab, our old neighbour, took care of one or two. Mahomet Biri the Tripoli Turk, the bearer of the first relief to Emin Pasha, took charge of some others; so that in this time of great trouble we received kindly sympathy and help from people of Islam.

After our first futile attempt to see Mwanga, the next morning Mackay and I went up again to his enclosure, taking with us the following letter written in the Luganda language :—

[*Translation of Letter.*]

"Natete, Oct. 26, 1885.

"MWANGA, KABAKA WA BUGANDA.
(MWANGA, KING OF UGANDA.)

"SEBO (SIR),

"We, the Englishmen, your guests, pray you to inform us concerning our brother, the bishop, who, we hear is at Luba's. We hear, moreover, that he is in danger. Therefore, sir, we pray you to send a messenger to extricate him, and to protect him efficiently."

This letter we signed, and it was duly delivered to the king. He sent out to say that he would send for the Baflansa (Frenchmen) to read it to him. We knew that this was another put off; he would not see us, how could he indeed. So sadly we came away. In the afternoon Père Lourdel came down and told us that he had seen the king, who commanded Mackay to come and write a letter to the bishop, telling him not to come by the Basoga road. Mackay had at this time a very bad attack of fever; but he immediataly wrote the letter, and I made all haste to take it up to the king's enclosure. Soon after I had arrived there, in walked Mackay. In spite of fever he had hurried after me on the donkey.

The king was only playing with us. We waited till nightfall and then returned, our darkest fears strengthened by what we were told, that the king had ordered the messengers not to return until they had killed the white men.

I quote from my journal, Monday, Oct. 26th, 1885 : " The king said, ' What can these (Mackay and I) do if I kill their brethren ? ' What, indeed, O righteous God ; but tell it unto Thee."

At one of his barazas Mwanga accused us of calling our place a royal enclosure. This may have arisen

from Mr. O'Flaherty saying one day in the merest jest
to Ndaula, the young king of Koki who used to visit
us, "Have you come to Kika"—a word used only of
coming to see the king. Rumours again became rife of
Mwanga's intention to murder all the Christian readers.
On the 5th of November, Père Lourdel, who had done
all he could to save the bishop, sent us a letter
confirming the sorrowful tidings of the death of
Hannington and all his porters, and telling us that we
were to be put to death also. That night one of
Mutesa's daughters, the "Mumbeja" (princess) Nalamansi, sent down to warn us to make friends with the
king at once, and to send a large present. Mackay and
I did so, sending a quantity of valuable things to the
king and the chief judge and Kyimbugwe. The king
accepted his, and the chief judge sent down to say that
we might now sleep in peace as he would protect us;
but Kyimbugwe sent to say we must send him some
more as our gift was not sufficient. So we sent him
a few more things.

The king, however, sent down a message to command
Mackay to come up at once to the Kibuga (palace).
We felt great uncertainty of what was in store for us,
and quite expected that orders would be given to put
us in the stocks.

When we arrived we found Père Lourdel was also
waiting, and the three of us were admitted into the
king's presence. To our no small surprise, he ordered
chairs to be brought for us, and we sat down.

There were present Kulugi and Kauta (chief cook), who was a young Mahometan and a faithful servant of Mwanga; he was afterwards burned to death, endeavouring to save his master's valuables in the great fire which destroyed Mwanga's enclosure. Kyimbugwe, now Pokino, Earl of Budu, was also present, a few pages were there as well—some of them our eager little scholars; and it was pleasant to know that though they dared not give us a smile of recognition, they were quite true to us.

The king began by saying to Mackay, "What is the meaning of the present you sent me?"

Mackay: "For friendship."

King: "What is your judgment?"

Reply: "It is not for judgment, it is for friendship."

King: "Have I only 'eaten Buganda' to-day, why give it me now, and not long ago?"

To this Mackay replied that he had finished repairing the king's gun. This was a little diversion, and the gun was brought for the king to look at—yes, it was very good—another gun which we had sent, and which had belonged to Mackay was brought. The king said, "Have you another gun?"

"No," replied Mackay, "I do not require a gun." Then Mwanga looked at it: "But how can I take your only gun? besides, see it is out of order—well, put it right, and send it to-morrow." But the king was eager to return to the matter of the present.

King: "Well now, the present, what is it for?"

I said, " We thought you were angry with us, because when we came to see you, you refused to see us."

Old Pokino now joined in, " Yes, and they sent me a present, and the Katikiro also, because they think we can influence the king. They think we want to kill them, and they wish to redeem their lives. What danger are they in ? Do we kill guests ? do we kill Baziba, or Basoga, or Arabs ?

It was contemptible of this old fellow so to turn against us, for he always professed himself our warm friend. I turned to him and said, " Why, then, did you send back to say our present was not large enough, and tell us to send you more ? " Pokino was nonplussed for a moment, and the others smiled a little at this. However they all began to rail against us. At last Mackay said, " Have we done wrong to give the king a present ? " This was a telling question, which nonplussed them again. Then I said, " You all know why we sent it. We want to hear about our brother." General chorus : " Who told you about your brother ? " " Answer : " Does not all Buganda know it ? " Chorus : " Oh, does all Buganda go to your place ? " Then the king addressed Kolugi and said, " Question them exceedingly ; " so we were pitilessly plied with questions. Some of our informants were sitting by us, Père Lourdel being the chief, also some of the little pages who used to keep us supplied with information. We put off our cross-examiners as well as we could ; finally we said, " We have not come here to ' ropa ' (inform on) people." Whereupon they

waxed angry, and the king called us hypocrites, and
added that we were "bagwagwa,"* the most insulting
term in the language. Manoga, the king's tailor, now
came back to the question of who had told us about the
Bishop. The king said, "They refuse to tell; because
they think I shall kill the person." Then he tried a
wheedling tone. "Tell me," he said, "and you will be
'baganze enyo' (great favourites)." Our continued
silence made them very wroth, and then came angry
words about killing. "What if I kill you?" said the
king. "What could Queeni (the Queen) do? Was
she able to touch Lukonge or Mirambo when they
killed white men? What could she do, or all Bulaya
(Europe) together? How would they come—would they
fly?" Père Lourdel now kindly attempted to create a
diversion in our favour. He said, "If you killed these
white men, then I should not care to stay in your
country." "If I killed them," insolently replied the
king, "should I spare you? Are you not a white man
like them?" The Père reflected on this in silence
during the remainder of the interview.

Mwanga then said he would not have the east road
used. Was he not the king? Who was Queeni?

We replied, "We are not messengers of Queeni, but
messengers of God." Then Kauta began to mock, and
they complained that we made the people our children,
which led to some coarse humour from Mwanga, the
first and last time I ever heard him say anything of

* Lowest of the low.

the sort. By this time we were thoroughly worried and harassed.* The king now addressed us directly, and appointed us "babaka" (king's messengers) to guard our own place, and to see that no people came near us—to see us or to sell us anything—and he added, "If you do not guard your place properly I will seize you and put you in the stocks." "Yes," added Kolugi, "and kill you."

Pokino now returned to his point, and said we lived in constant fear of our lives, and that we could neither eat nor sleep. "Well, look at us," I said, "and say if we appear like people who live as you say, and who fear to be killed." They then turned on me. "What brought you to Buganda, and who asked you to come? Mackay we want, but what can you do?" I said, "I thought you desired teachers, and Mutesa sent his canoes for me." They then took up the question of our teaching, and wanted to know why we did not teach the king and the chiefs. "Why," they scornfully asked, "did you not teach Kataluba (one of Wilson and Felkin's envoys) when he went to Europe? And why do you not teach your own Wagwana (servants)?"

More than two hours of this ceaseless attack had passed, and we were quite tired out, while no conclusion had been arrived at.

Suddenly Mwanga called an attendant, and said, "Take these white men and give them two cows to quiet their

---

* Mr. O'Flaherty had been treated in the same way by the Katikiro; and sent with Mujasi to search our house, see p. 143.

minds;" and then he dismissed the court. And so we
went home with our cows, devoutly thankful to God
for having brought us through such an unpleasant
ordeal.

During this time of deep trouble, when people dare
only come to us by stealth or at night, the young
Admiral Gabunga sent a message to say that he wished
to be baptised, and a day or two afterwards a letter
came from Duta—one of the native church council—to
say that Gabunga and some of his people had come
down to Walukaga's enclosure, and that some other
members of the church council were assembled there,
and wished the young chief to be baptised. This boy
had always stuck to us, and used to come in state with
all his retinue, and dressed in his scarlet coat on
Sundays, and he never was ashamed of the fact of his
being a reader. We decided to comply with his desire,
and I then went to Walukaga's and performed the rite,
being the only available clergyman. Mr. O'Flaherty,
the only other ordained missionary, all this time had
been far from well, and the worry and anxiety of this
terrible time had brought on severe fever, from which
he never really recovered. Mwanga allowed him to
leave at the end of the year, and on his way home in
the following July, 1886, he died in the Red Sea.
Requiescat in pacem.

Walukaga was a most remarkable man. He was
the king's head blacksmith, and one of the most intelligent Africans I have ever known. Mackay, when

making Namasole's coffin, became acquainted with him and liked him, and a friendship sprang up between them. Walukaga afterwards visited Mackay, and listened most attentively to what he told him. It was the revealing of a new and wonderful idea to him, and the opening up of a hope transcending far anything of which he had ever before dreamed. And he cried out, "How is it when we were making Namasole's coffin you told me none of these good things?"

If the teaching of that blacksmith alone had been all that Mackay had accomplished (which it was not), yet even in that case who would dare to say his years of self-sacrificing toil and frequent fevers and unceasing worries had been endured in vain!

Walukaga was a splendid Christian according to my ideas. Yet, according to some English Christians, Christ's teaching was too high for him and such as he.

Some days later Duta again wrote conveying a serious piece of news. His letter ran as follows :—

"We have heard that yesterday the king was in a bad way. Bwana Mapera (Lourdel) gave him medicine for his eyes, and told him not to rub them with oil. Well, at night the king did rub them with oil, and called the Katikiro and all the chiefs, and said to them 'The white men have given me poison, I am in an evil plight.' And all the people wept much, and they said the white men want to kill the king, and now he is ill. But this news is very bad, etc., etc." The same day news reached us that Balikudembe—a young chief who learned to read at our mission, but who joined the French priest's pupils afterwards—had been seized, and that he was under sentence of death by fire.

"That afternoon a whole troop of pages came down from Mwanga bringing 8000 cowrie shells, as part payment for some things which he had bought from us. One of the boys, Tito, drew me aside and told me that Balikudembe was dead. This young hero had dared to tell the tyrant that he did unwisely to kill the white men. Mwanga forthwith sent for the chancellor. "See!" he said, "this fellow wants to insult me," and then the cruel death-sentence was passed. The chief executioner was a friend of Balikudembe's, and mercifully killed him with a sword before committing his body to the flames.

Soon after this, moved by some restless impulse, I went to visit the spot where Lugalama died. It was late, about 1 A.M., as I made my way to the dismal swamp, the scene of that sorrowful tragedy. Once before I had visited the place with a faithful friend, Musali. He and I knelt there and I bade him pray, for I could find no words. He did pray—prayed for the murderer, and prayed for his fellow-countrymen. He himself was soon to die for his faith, true Christian indeed, although of the race for whom Islam is good enough!

This night, however, I went alone. There was a brilliant moon, casting inky shadows and revealing the

weird shapes of the plantain trees with their silvery
leaves. I could hear the ceaseless sound of innumerable crickets, yet except for this there was an awful
silence and stillness. The way led past four cross
roads over the brow of a hill, and down to the valley
where the swamp called Mayanja lay, and to which I
was going. At the cross roads was a sacred building,
which I entered and knelt down. Then I came out
and went on. That sorrowful procession which had
passed this very road only a year before seemed to be
with me now, and I the saddest of them all. The
path dipped down to the edge of the swamp. I
descended the hill and entered the chill and murky
atmosphere of the morass and came to the very place.
It had evidently been lately used. There was the
framework of rough branches charred and blackened,
and some of them fallen. The frame-work on which
the mutilated bodies of some other unhappy victims
had been fixed quivering over the slow flame.

As I stood there my stick struck something hard, and
I stooped down and picked up the object which lay at
my feet—a human skull. I stood there gazing at it, and
again the awful question of the meaning of the mystery
of life and death came upon me. I put the skull
gently down again, and turned away and made my
way homewards, relieved, I think, by this pilgrimage.

On the 3rd of December, 1886, I took to the king
a letter from Egypt for Emin Pasha. Sir John Kirk
had asked us to endeavour to prevail upon Mwanga to

SCENE OF LUGALAMA'S DEATH.

To face p. 206.

forward letters to Emin. The king received the letter, and a little later sent it on.

The new year saw things brighter. Mr. O'Flaherty had been allowed to leave in peace, and Mwanga continued to be civil. He sent a present to Mackay one day of 10,000 cowries, telling him he was a muganze (favourite).

Very soon afterwards he gave Mackay another 8000 cowries, and sent a polite demand for my trousers. He had fallen in love with them, when I swam for him. I complied with his request and sent him a pair.

At the beginning of the year Mwanga had sent out an enormous raiding expedition against Bunyoro, of which Kangao, ruler of Bulemezi, was in command. On the 5th of February a letter reached us from the Russian traveller, Dr. Junker, from the north. He was in ignorance of events at Khartoum, but was desirous of coming to Uganda en route for the coast. Mackay immediately went and told Mwanga of the traveller's position, taking a present to the king. Mackay explained who Junker was; but the king said that when he heard that a white man was with Kabarega he had immediately sent to attack him. However, he ordered Mackay to return next day, who promised both the king and Katikiro a present of some cartridges, which seemed to put them into high good humour. On the following day an important council of chiefs was held, and they decided, at Mackay's request, to send to Kangao the general of the Uganda armies to order him to protect Junker.

On the 19th of February Mahomet Biri returned from Bunyoro, whither he had been, and brought Emin's and Junker's mail, which they wished us to forward. Junker wrote to us, telling of his desire to come our way; he also wrote to the king in Arabic.

The next day Mackay went up with the letters which had arrived from the north, and gave the Katikiro the letter which Emin had written to him. Mackay also spoke to Mwanga of Emin; but the king seemed much more interested in the coat which Mackay was wearing, and which he coveted, than in the matters of Emin Pasha. It seemed to please Mwanga to treat any other ruler with as much contempt as possible.

A few days later an occurrence took place which we feared might lead to a general massacre of Christians.

In the evening while we were at prayers we suddenly saw a strange glow in the sky, and unable to restrain their curiosity the boys ran out to see what it was, and they came back saying, "Kibuga Kiyide," the palace is in flames. Suddenly there was a loud report —" Mizinga," cannon, they exclaim—then another, and another—" Baruana," they are fighting, was now the cry. There was great excitement; the reports, however, were dull, and more like the blowing up of gunpowder, which it turned out to be, than the report of small cannon. With characteristic caution the Kabaka kept his stores of gunpowder in a straw-built house in which a fire was continually burning. After a while a lad belonging to the chancellor came down and told us that the whole kibuga (enclosure) was destroyed. A little later Entanda Gideon appeared; he had lately distinguished himself by dropping two of Mwanga's best guns into the Nyanza, where they were lost. Mwanga, to his great credit be it said, did not punish him in any way; but Gideon's story now was, that he and Samweli and the other assistant store-keepers had gone behind the house, according to their nightly custom, to have prayers, leaving the store-house unoccupied, except by a wee Mukedi boy named " Bina." The fire was burning brightly, presently during prayers an enterprising spark floated up and caught on a cobweb in the roof, a straw was ignited from this and burst into a tiny flame. In another minute the straw roof was ablaze. Back rushed the boys and made frantic efforts to extinguish the fire, but the fire was master; wildly they seized the different things of which they were the custodians and rushed out with them. But the great straw-built dome was a sheet of living flame, and the high wind soon carried masses of blazing grass to the next house, where a still larger quantity of gunpowder was stored; it too soon was a sheet of flame, and as the small barrels of powder exploded, burning brands were blown in all directions, and soon the whole of the vast royal enclosure was roaring to destruction. Far off it was a splendid sight: it must have been truly magnificent close at hand.

P

The young Mahometan head cook, Kauta, distinguished himself by his reckless daring in endeavouring to save his master's property, in doing which he sustained fatal injuries; as also another chief called Mulamba—the little child Bina was also burned to death. The splendid donkey which Mwanga had taken from us some weeks before perished in the flames.

Mwanga, when he saw the fire, jumped to the conclusion that it was caused by rebels, and that what, I suppose he daily expected, had happened, namely that the whole country was in rebellion, and that the rebels had fired his capital. Seizing a naked sword he rushed from his flaming palace, followed by some dozen of his boys, these he bade strip off their white garments that they might not be discernible, and then fled away into the darkness. Père Lourdel, the French priest, having seen the fire, at once made his way up to the court [he was allowed by Mwanga to use a private road], and suddenly came upon the flying monarch. He stopped him and tried to reassure him. At this juncture some of the chiefs came up and conducted Mwanga to the Katikiro's enclosure.

The chancellor's store-house was soon struck by lightning. Kiwanuka, the God of Thunder, could not allow the divine Kabaka to be driven out of his houses by fire without sending a thunderbolt into the Katikiro's enclosure—at any rate, both times that the king's enclosure was burnt the Katikiro's place was on fire immediately afterwards.

The king then said that he would go to the
Nyanza, where the chief Edward (Mulyagonja) had
built him another straw palace. This the chancellor
opposed on the ground that Kabarega would hear of it,
and say that Mwanga had fled from fear of him.
Kabarega, we were told, *planted* a man and a baboon—
i.e. buried them alive in the road by which the enemy
would reach him, as a sacrifice or spell to bewitch the
Baganda armies. I am sure Kabarega must have
prided himself on the success of his charm, for in the
fighting which ensued the Muganda Generalissimo
Kangao was killed, as well as many of the Baganda
people. The Banyoro getting far the best of the
battle.

At the end of February, 1886, a report reached us
that Mwanga had ordered Bilali, the overseer of the
markets, to seize people who came to us to learn.
Nothing, however, came of it.

Mwanga was gradually becoming disagreeable again.
He had said after the fire that the white men had
bewitched him, and would be the death of him some
day. He also said that he knew he should be the last
black king of Buganda. About this time he gave his
head hangman, Mukajangwa, orders to kill Mackay if
he brought the boat to a certain place where Mwanga
had himself ordered him to bring it. The king bade
this executioner take men and cut off Mackay's head
and bring his hat to the enclosure. Mackay heard of it,
and did not go to the forbidden spot; and the chancellor,

hearing of the order, sent down to Mackay to warn
him not to go. But things of this sort were only the
precursors of a coming storm.

About this time we sent off Emin's letters by one of
Gabunga's people who was going south in canoes,
while Mackay was visiting the king at Munyonyo,
quite near the lake. At this place we had a small
grass house near the royal enclosure, and we took it in
turns to attend the king's baraza. Mackay had several
interviews with him, in one of which Mwanga remarked
that if the " Balozi " (Consul at Zanzibar) were to write
seventy letters for him, he should not allow him to
leave the country.

This point of being allowed to come and go at will
was one which we were always trying in a quiet way
to gain.

A few days later I went down and had one of my
last interviews with Mwanga.

After dismissing the general baraza (levée), he called
Kulugi and me back again. I had brought some of
our little reading books, which I showed him. He
asked if the printing was done with iron. I said that
it was, and he remarked that nearly all the wonderful
things of the Bazungu (Europeans) were made with
iron. I asked him when he was going to read, and
told him that our Queen, though so great and mighty,
was a humble Christian. This set him off about the
Prince of Wales. He tried to say his name. I said
it slowly, and he repeated it after me. Again return-

ing to the subject of religion, I asked him what a
man really had if he had no life from God after death.
He replied by asking me if I had any scarlet shoes such
as are worn by Turks; and then if I knew anything
about the white man (Junker) who wished to come to
Buganda. I said I did not. He asked if he were an
Englishman. I said, "No, a Murusi—Russian." After
this conversation, I went to see the chancellor. He
hated me, but was generally freezingly polite—never
more. I believe Mackay was the only European that
he could endure.

Next day, Kagwa (Apolo), one of our converts, now a
trusted servant of the king, sent a little boy named
Lulè down to me with a paper. It had belonged to
Bishop Hannington—a blank letter of orders—" We,
James, by Divine permission Bishop of the Church of
England in Eastern Equatorial Africa," &c. Lulè said
he must take it back, as it might be missed.

About the middle of April, Mackay again visited
Mwanga. He had not done so for many weeks after
the king's order to have him killed. When Mackay
went in, Mwanga began begging for cartridges. Mackay
reproached the king for treating him as an enemy,
saying, "The more we give you, the more you hate us."
"What proof do you offer of that?" said the king.
"What order did you give to Mukajangwa?" asked
Mackay. "Who told you about that?" said the king.
"Is it not true?" answered Mackay.

Lukoto, an inferior Judge, happened to be there;

and the king said : "Kale tuwoze musango "—"Let us
plead our case."

Kulugi, who was present, then began to state the case
for the king ; and when he was silent, Mackay stated
his side. When he had finished, Kulugi said : "Gutu-
sinze"—"The judgment goes against us," or "over-
comes us."

Mackay then left Munyonyo, and came back to
Natete, the mission station ; and the next Sunday,
Easter-day, there was a report that the Christians
were to be seized, and so they were afraid to assemble
in any numbers. Twenty, however, came to the communion in the morning ; and in the afternoon ten more
came for the same purpose ; and in the evening, fifteen
more faithful people came to the Lord's Supper, made
more solemn than ever by the fact of the rumour of the
morning. There were some there who partook of it
for the last time before dying for the faith, of which
it is a symbol.

CHAPTER XVIII.

BAGANDA CONVERTS AND MARTYRS.

THIS month we obtained a new acquisition in Mwana awulira, a young slave whom we redeemed. Bikweyamba, a scion of the royal family of Bunyoro and a Muganda chief, had lately been seized and put in the stocks on the charge of not bringing in sufficient tribute to the king. He was a friend of mine, and sent his sister, Narwaga, a Mumbeja, or princess, to beg for cloth to pay his guards in order to mitigate his confinement. He was heavily loaded with the "kaligo" (slave fork), and had his feet and hands in the stocks, "emvuba." By paying a certain amount he could release a hand, and by paying still more a foot until he was entirely free. Now to raise money he had been selling his slaves to the Arabs. I told Narwaga that if her brother wanted cloth he had better send one of his slaves to us and we would take him in pawn, and if he liked his slave back he might return the cloth and get him out. I had already given some cloth, but did not wish to be troubled by his asking every day for more. I knew very well that he would never send for his boy again, for the price I was giving was several yards more than he was worth.

A day or two later Narwaga said to the slave boy, "Come and let us visit the white men." She did not say I have sold you for thirty-six yards of cloth. So he got up and followed her. He was a Muhangiro, or Mujangiro, from the south-west of the Nyanza, I suppose about 14 years old, slightly lame, having six toes on one foot. · Let him tell his own story :—*

"When I got to the Bazungu's house I saw some strange things. Two outlandishly dressed white men, who kept their fire on a large board which they ate off. They had large black clubby sort of feet; their toes, unlike ordinary people's, were all together in one. I was utterly bewildered by the way which these people ate their food. I could see long things protruding from their hands; could they be nails or some strange growth peculiar to Bazungu? They gave me plenty of food, and then a lot of people followed one of the Bazungu and we climbed up into the roof, or rather into another house, on the top of the one in which they ate their food, and then they began to sing; I never heard singing like that before, and I did not like it much. Then they stopped and every one knelt down, and I did too, and the Bazungu began to say words, praying to some one, some great chief, but I could see no one but ourselves. My mistress then told me I was to stay there. I did not mind much, for there were other boys, and I soon got used to the

---

* I give the boy's own words.

new life." The fire which Mwana awulira saw on the board was our lamp on the table.

Mackay on one occasion while on the lake had a ship's lamp with a globe—it was nice and bright. A native of Sesse, seeing the lamp on the ground, and wishing to light his fire, brought a bunch of dried grass and thrust it to the glass which he did not see, and waited a second, then tried again, and found it a complete failure; he said, in a tone of great disgust, "Eh, omuliro gwa muzungu guganye." "Eugh! the fire of the white man refuses," and went elsewhere to seek a more accommodating flame.

Our new boy's former master had given him the name Mudu awulira, the obedient slave. I called him Mwana awulira, the obedient child. He eventually came with me to Zanzibar.

I make an extract here from my diary of May 1st, 1886 :—

Evil tidings reached us to-day; the faithful Musali or Kidza came and told us that Mwanga had been storming about the number of readers who were learning, so we warned our friends not to come about us. We have heard several times lately rumours of evil, and the storm which had been so long brewing broke at last in awful fury upon the Christian readers of both denominations, Protestant and Roman Catholic. On the 22nd of May Semfuma Tomasi came and told us two items of news: First, that Nalamansi, the Christian Mumbeja, had given great offence by flinging

away all her sacred charms, "mayembe," and by burning her ancestral relics. And the other, that a nice
quiet lad named Matia, who had lately been baptised,
had dared, though indirectly, to disobey the commands
of the king. This boy was the son of the chief Mugula,
and himself held the office of Sabagabo in the Kitongole
of the " bagalagala," or pages.

A Mahometan reader, Kawuta, head cook and a considerable chief, made the request at Mwanga's baraza
that the page Sabagabo should be handed over to him
for an evil purpose, to which the king acceded. Sabagabo, however, bravely stood out against the shameful
treatment to which the chief wished to subject him.
And it was this splendid act of disobedience which,
when reported to Mwanga, served to set the spark to
the train which had already been laid.

The next day, Alexandro Namfumbambi, now Mutebe
—his new chieftanship—came and told us that Sabagabo
had been badly beaten, and was lying in the stocks.
And then we heard the terrible news that the Christian
readers had been seized and many of them put to death.
Nyonyi Entono, my friend (a Roman Catholic reader),
who now held a most important office, " Musalo-salo,"
was cruelly and shamefully mutilated by the orders of
the king. He recovered, and afterwards actually became
katikiro, or chief judge, in place of the haughty chancellor. That functionary killed two of his pages who had
been seen reading. The same day Kagwa (Apolo) was
called into the king's presence with another youth; a

stormy scene ensued. The king, acting on an impulse of uncontrollable fury, attacked the other lad with a spear, gashing him frightfully, and he was hurried away and murdered by the executioners. Then the king turned to Apolo : "Are you a reader?" he cried, trembling with passion. "Nsoma, Mukamawange," "I read, my Lord," was the brave reply. "Then I'll teach you to read!" shouted the angry king, and gashed him too with the spear, and then took the wooden handle and broke it over his back. At last, breathless with the exertion, his anger having apparently spent itself, he told him to begone. And Kagwa's life was saved, and no more was done to him. He afterwards rose to be Mukwenda in the latest revolution.

The noble blacksmith, Walukaga, was seized, and the faithful Musali. Alexandro Namfumbambi, who often gave us trouble by his inconsistencies, on hearing of the seizure of his fellow-Christians, went boldly up to the court, and when the executioners asked if any readers were concealed in his enclosure, replied, "I myself am a Christian;" and was at once apprehended and made prisoner.

On the morning of this dismal day, I was sitting in a kind of verandah at the back of the mission house, and a number of people were seated round learning their letters. We had just been singing a hymn—

"Bona bona bakusinza   =   "All the people bow before Thee,

Gwe Kakaba wo mugulu"   Thou the Ruler of the heavens"—

when Mackay suddenly appeared. He came up to where I was sitting, and said in English: " I have just heard that the king has gone mad and given orders to seize all the Christians." The readers saw our troubled looks, and we turned and told them what it was. I said to them, "Escape quickly lest they search our place;" and they hurried off and made their way out through a hole in our back fence. They had hardly gone when Bilali, a coastman in the king's service, came with an armed following to search for Christians. He conducted his search in a very gentlemanly way saying he was sorry to have to trouble us. He found no one, since they had all effected their escape.

The next news which we heard was that Monseigneur Lavinhac, the French Vicar Apostolique, had just arrived from the south of the Nyanza with another priest. He had taught Mwanga at a former time, and we hoped that his influence might prove of some avail in saving the lives of the poor people now in prison.

But so far from this being the case, Mwanga signalised the coming of the French bishop by killing several of the Frenchmen's most prominent pupils. He caused to be mutilated also one of our converts, a young sub-chief named Musamula, who soon died from the effects of his cruelty. This young man had been a follower of Mwanga when the king was still a " mulangira" (prince). One day his master ordered him to go and " nyagga" (steal) some goats; he refused, since he was learning to be a Christian, so was instantly dismissed from

Mwanga's service. I advised him to return and make it up, which he did, and was received back. When Mwanga became king, he gave Embwa (the dog), for that was his name, the small chieftainship of Kisamula, when he assumed the name of Musamula.

The king gave orders that three of Namesole's (queen mother) pages should be put to death, which was carried out. Daily we heard of the murder of some one of our converts; but strange to say, Sabagabo, the boy whose bravery had immediately led to this terrible outbreak, was liberated. The very last time I was at Mengo, Mwanga's capital, I saw him. He dared not say much to me, as there were generally spies about who would quickly report any one seen speaking to the dreaded Bazungu. Latterly we hardly dared to notice our friends lest we should mark them, and thus lead to their being persecuted.

The 27th of May a very likely and alarming report reached us that the mission was to be sacked. Our boys were in great consternation. "*Sauve qui peut*" was all that we could say to them, and Mackay and I were left alone. Our coast servants had never been touched, and so they did not leave us. But they did not live in our enclosure or compound, so that we two were practically alone. It was a dark day. Mackay wrote to the French bishop, suggesting that all the Europeans should adopt some concerted plan of action; but he replied that he did not think it advisable, and possibly he was right. The chiefs were in an angry and irritated frame of mind; yet we could not bear the thought of passively sitting down without making some effort to save those Christians who were still alive, though under sentence of death.

The Katikiro sent three times to demand that Mugoa, a young chief who had lately been advanced by the king, should be killed. Twice the king refused, but the imperious chancellor seemed to be again in the ascendant, and would take no denial. He would not eat until the murdered chief's hand was brought to him, to show that his orders had been carried out.

The king, in order to revenge himself on the chancellor for murdering Mugoa, sent to demand the life of Sebwato, a prominent Christian, whom I have mentioned as the captor and master and liberator of Lugalama. The Katikiro sent back to say that he would see that Sebwato was dealt with. He was most useful to the chancellor, and was a faithful and discreet servant, who managed his master's business transactions with the Arabs of Karagwe. Sebwato was commanded to appear before the chief judge, and questioned as to his connection with the foreign superstition. He said little, but he was notoriously a Christian, and so the Katikiro commanded him to be beaten publicly, which order was carried out. Sebwato took his castigation patiently. He was a tender-hearted man, and I recollect his being moved to tears, when he and I were speaking of the death of our little friend Lugalama. Sebwato subsequently gained great glory in battle. One of the charges brought against Christians was, that they would not fight for their king, nor put bullets in their guns. However, in one of the encounters in which the Baganda were engaged, Sebwato greatly distinguished himself by his valour, and then the Baganda said there were none so brave as the Christians.

After the murder of the bishop I had said to the chancellor: "If you do not wish us to be here, let us go." To me he made no reply. Père Lourdel had seen him also, and begged of him, if there was anything wrong in our teaching, to drive us away; "but do not kill your own children," he urged. "No," replied the chancellor; "you are guests, and we will not drive you away; but as many as you teach we shall kill." It was this determination on the part of the chiefs which led Mackay and me to decide to ask for permission to leave the country. We felt that if they once saw that we were not staying on against their will, which they often implied that we were doing, they would be more likely, not only to abstain from killing our converts, but also to urge us to remain.

The next convert of whom I shall speak, though not a martyr, deserves mention; I refer to the old sub-chief Isaya, of Kasengeje, a place bright in the Christian annals of Buganda as being the home of quite a com-

munity of " Bamasiya " Christians. The head of this
community, Isaya, had been deposed from his chieftainship of Munakulya, and succeeded in it by Masudi, a
renegade one-eyed Arab.[*]

I shall never forget old Isaya visiting Mackay at
dead of night. It was after the wholesale murder of
many of the Christians, and some of his lads, retainers
and slaves, were under sentence of death. He came
and told Mackay about it; and when he reached this
point—that his people were to be seized—he said:
"They are going to kill my children! my children!"
and burst into uncontrollable tears. Mackay did all
he could to soothe and comfort him. As a matter of
fact, however, his people were not molested.

On the 29th of May Mackay visited the king, who
was still at Munyonyo, and begged for the lives of the
Christians who were under sentence in prison. The
king promised to spare them, but did not keep his
word.

The next day I went to Munyonyo. On the side of
the road as I passed there was a human head, which
looked as if it had been carefully placed there after
being severed from the trunk. It had a sort of fascination for me. I tried to discern the features, but it was
the face of no one whom I knew. A little further, on
the other side of the road, were the limbs hacked in

---

[*] Masudi was present at Bishop Hannington's capture. He was
one of that insolent drunken set through whom Hannington passed
with a high hand.

pieces at the joints. I went on, sick at heart. I arrived too late, and was not admitted to the king's baraza. While sitting outside in the storehouse, I was told of the death of Mukasa, a bright brave boy, who on one occasion had administered a thorough thrashing to a companion who was leading some of the younger pages astray. His Christian name was Musa; he was one of the first killed. He was murdered at the door of Walukaga's smithy. I heard, too, the story of Walukaga's capture. When they came to seize him, his wife Hannah, a most intelligent woman and clever reader, escaped with the rest of the household; but he stood firm, and was taken. He waited for a definite reason, and it was this: The Christians were suspected of disloyalty and sedition. Now the most prominent of them would not run away nor go into hiding, lest they should give colour to this suspicion. They appealed to the laws of their country, and were prepared "Kuwoza Musango," to plead for judgment, before the proper tribunal. It was this spirit and this confidence in the righteousness of their cause which so puzzled the rulers, and which made the Christians such a power in the country.

Then followed the crowning act in the cruel tragedy, when Walukaga and some thirty others met their heroic deaths. A mighty pyre was heaped about the Christian captives. Each was firmly bound, a burning brand was brought, and soon the consuming fire enfolded this company of saints, of whom the world was not worthy;

Q

and so calling, if report speaks truly, on their persecutors to believe in Christ, they were caught away in their chariot of flame.

A little later and we heard of the death of Musali Kidza, who had been warned by his master the Mujasi to make his escape; but, like Walukaga, he refused to do so. He was accordingly taken; the unrighteous sentence was pronounced, and they dashed his brains out with a club, and this was the manner of his martyrdom.

At the time of this horrible butchery the mission premises were utterly deserted. However, Namutwe, the old chief from whom I had bought little Jimmy, sent down a number of children to be vaccinated. They came in charge of a small boy, Kiwobe (death-wail), who had learned to read fluently under the instruction of one of the members of the Native Church Council named Munyaga bye nju. While Mackay was vaccinating the children, Kiwobe came to me and said, "Munange njagala kubatizibwa"—"My friend, I wish to be baptised." This was a most extraordinary request at such a time. His teacher, Munyaga, had just been murdered in the most shockingly frightful manner. I cannot forbear to tell the story :—

When Munyaga was captured he was in his house actually teaching at the time. The little party of readers saw the " Bamboa," executioners, coming up the slope of the hill on which stood the house, where they were. Immediately there was a stampede, and the

lads and others escaped. But Munyaga, like Walukaga,
would not fly, but sat where he was and waited. The
executioners came cautiously up. They saw a gun
leaning against the reed lintel of the door and stopped,
hesitating, believing it was the possession of a loaded
gun that gave Munyaga such confidence. He, seeing their
evident fear, told them they need not be afraid of the gun,
for he did not mean to use it. So they came up to ap-
prehend him. He begged to be allowed to put on his
"kansu" (white gown), which they agreed to, and then
they led him away. His trial was a cruel mockery,
and he was ordered to be hacked in pieces and burned.
His torturers cut off one of his arms and flung it into
the fire before him, then they cut off a leg, and that,
too, was flung into the flame, and lastly, the poor
mutilated body was laid on the framework to be consumed. Ashes to ashes, dust to dust, in sure and
certain hope of the resurrection of the dead.

Now to return to young Kiwobe's request for
baptism: "Do you know what you are asking?" I said
to him. "Mmanyi munange"—"I know, my friend," he
replied. "But," I said, "you know if you say you are
a Christian they would kill you." Again he said the
same words, "I know, my friend." "But," I said,
"suppose people asked you if you were a reader, would
you tell a lie and deny it and say no?" He replied,
"Ndiyatula munange"—"I shall confess, my friend."
Mackay and I both thought he was worthy of the rite,
for he had a good knowledge of reading and seemed to

Q 2

have been well taught, so he was baptised there and then. He chose the name of Samweli.

The first Samuel * baptised was the "Mapera boy." His native name was Mukasa, but Mutesa called him Muganze Awongererwa, the favourite who was asked of the gods, so I thought "Samuel," or "Samweli," would be an appropriate Christian name.

When Samuel grew to be about eighteen, and the election of the Native Church Council took place, though he was the youngest candidate, he was elected with only one dissentient vote. Walukaga, I think, was the only member unanimously chosen. .

Samweli, Kagwa (Apolo), and Waswa, another Christian, were keepers of the king's stores, under Kolugi, and Samweli had been appointed just before this time to go into Busongora to collect the king's tribute of cowrie shells. While he was away this frightful persecution had broken out, and his was one of the principal names in the fatal proscription. The king was only waiting for his return to have him killed. On his way back he learned the terrible news of the cruel murder of his fellow-Christians, and of the fell intention regarding himself.

I was awakened at about 3 A.M. one morning by a low knocking at the door—it is pitch dark in Buganda at that hour—and on getting up and striking a light,

---

* It was this young man, with others, who came to Stanley's camp on the west of the Nyanza, and of whom the great traveller wrote in high terms. (Letter in *Times*, Jan. 7th, 1890.)

I found Samweli and Semfuma of Kasengeje, together
with Samweli's little step-brother, Ali Wali, and one
or two others. I admitted them and lighted the lamp,
and then they told me what they had come for.
Samweli was naturally in great trouble, and asked
what he should do. His companions had urged him
to fly for his life; but he was on the king's service,
and he could not feel it right to leave his trust, and so
he came to consult me.

My decision was soon given. "The king has not the
heart of a man, but of a wild beast," I said; "and you
are not bound to submit yourself to one who is so vile
a murderer. You are perfectly justified in forsaking
the trust." Semfuma went over to Mackay's house and
roused him up, and his verdict was the same as mine.
Semfuma was an "elder" also, and he had urged
Samweli to fly.

Samweli sat on the ground looking troubled and
dissatisfied, and then asked for a pencil and paper, and
bent over his paper and wrote. I am sorry now that I
did not keep that bit of paper. However, I said, "You
need not write; but tell me what you think." Then he
looked up and said, "Munange Siyinza okuleka ebintu
ebya kabaka," "My friend, I cannot leave the things of
the kabaka." The others began to urge on him the folly of
his intention, but I said, "No, he is right; he has spoken
well; he must take the tribute." Then we prayed
together, and we arranged that Samweli should try and
get his men to start early, that he might deposit the

loads of cowries at the enclosure of the chief appointed to receive them. This was in order that he might be released of his trust before the executioners were abroad in their search. He said sadly that he was afraid the " Baziba " carriers would not bestir themselves till long after daylight, and then he said good-bye. I wondered if I should ever see this young hero again.

A few days later, to my great delight, he appeared at nightfall, and told us how he had gone boldly to the enclosure of the chief and had deposited the loads, and had then walked out. I said, "You ran when you got outside." He said, "No; for I should have been noticed at once; I walked quite slowly till I got out of sight, and then I ran as quickly as I could, and so I escaped."

The Hon. Roden Noel has kindly allowed me to reproduce here a little poem which he has written on the above incident. It is called " Weak Things of the World," and is taken from his book entitled ' A Modern Faust.'

> " A Christian convert, a boy African,
>   Knowing the bloody lord of his great clan
>   Sought him to visit with a lingering death,
>   Because he had embraced Christ, humbly saith
>   To a revered white teacher urging flight,
>   He may not bend his soul to feel it right;
>   For, since he hath been commissioned by the king
>   Ingathered tribute from the tribes to bring
>   Home to the sovereign—coin of cowrie shells—
>   Whatever cruel personal peril dwells
>   Among those evil courts, how dare he thrust
>   From him the fatal honour of his trust :

And so he braves the tyrant. Ah, young black,
Spurned as inferior, thou hast e'en put back
Poor human nature on the pedestal
Whence pale dishonour dragged it to base fall.
The lowest whom men trample as the clod
Is of the royal family of God ;
The weakest woman sits enthroned above
The proud and wise by dignity of love;
Who liveth well alone hath found the key
To every dim, mind-baffling mystery."

CHAPTER XIX.

On the 2nd of June, 1886, Dr. Junker arrived at the mission house. Mwanga had given him leave to take up his abode with his fellow-Bazungu (Europeans), and we were able to let him occupy the upstairs rooms of the larger mission house. He brought us interesting news of Emin Pasha, and discussed the best means of sending him temporary relief. Emin had written saying he thought of sending his people in "little flocks" *via* Uganda to the coast. Mackay, who is a good German scholar, wrote a letter in German to Emin, warning him of Mwanga's treachery, and strongly advising him to stay where he was. Dr. Junker told us of the ghastly sights he had witnessed on reaching Buganda. He had seen many mutilated corpses lying by the wayside, for there had been a kind of inquisition held, and the various chiefs were obliged to give up a certain number of people to be killed for being "readers." It did not matter much whether they actually were readers, so long as the tale of murdered persons was complete. The young Christian Admiral did what he thought rather a clever thing; he gave up an innocent young goat-herd to be killed as a Christian, though the poor

child had never heard of such a thing as Christianity.
The little chief was very penitent when I told him how
wrong this was; and had he known that he was acting
improperly, would, I feel sure, not have done so. He
himself always confessed and admitted that he was a
Christian, but he was not powerful enough to screen his
dependents who were fellow-Christians without sacri-
ficing one of them. The young admiral afterwards lost
his own life in the same cause. This incident shows
how very small is the value the Baganda people and
Africans generally set upon human life. It is very
pathetic the thought of that poor little, unknown, un-
cared-for goat-herd dying unwept, a slave in a strange
land. Yet how strange that, whoever he is, he has
been counted worthy to die in Christ's cause.

When Dr. Junker was with us, the French Bishop
Lavinhac and Père Lourdel came and paid us a visit.
Dr. Junker very unselfishly offered to go with us and
protest in the name of humanity against the massacres,
and to demand instant leave for the eight Europeans
—five Frenchmen, Dr. Junker, Mackay, and myself—
to leave the country. The Frenchmen did not think
this advisable, and after all it was none of Dr. Junker's
business, and Mackay and I did not feel it right to
involve him in our troubles. Still, the intrepid traveller
was willing to cast in his lot with us; but the Frenchmen settled the difficulty by declining to act with us
in the matter, and as I said, referring to the former
occasion, possibly wisely.

Dr. Junker in a few days got together a present for Mwanga of various articles, and he and Mackay went over to Munyonyo, where the king still was holding his court. The capital at Mengo, which had been burnt, was being rebuilt, and was now rapidly approaching completion. Before Dr. Junker and Mackay had reached the enclosure at Munyonyo, Mwanga sent Kibare, a great chief, to tell them to return; for the king was soon going back to Mengo, where he would receive his new guests with proper honours. After some days the king returned, and Dr. Junker went up with Mackay to pay his respects. The king received him in full baraza (levée), and at Mackay's request consented to allow Dr. Junker to leave the country in the *Eleanor* (or *Mirembe*), our mission boat.

Then came on the matter of Emin Pasha and his letters: the first asking for permission to come through Buganda with all his people; the second only asking that a small party might have leave to pass. There was a great deal of whispering among the king and chiefs, and the renegade Arab, Masudi, mentioned previously, had a good deal to say, and insolently remarked that all Bazungu (white men) were liars. Soon after, a powerful Mahometan chief, Ntanda by name, came to demand from Junker Turkish slippers for the king—the red slippers which Mwanga had on a former occasion asked me about. Dr. Junker had only some of Khartoum manufacture, which he produced, but which the chief kicked contemptuously away. Junker then retired to his quarters, leaving the insolent messenger sitting in the verandah outside.

Not long after Junker had left the country, the French Bishop Lavinhac and Père Jeraud, a very quiet, amiable man, who had not been very long in Buganda, also obtained permission to leave. They paid us a farewell visit. Père Jeraud came to a tragic end. He was a very clever mechanic, and when at the south of the Nyanza, built a boat. While in her one day with some of his lads, he saw a hippopótamus, and having a gun with him, he determined to try a shot. A coastman, Mungwana, who accompanied him, advised him not, since the gun which he had was useless against such an enormous antagonist; but he fired at the unwieldy brute, his shot took effect, and the great creature came at the boat open-mouthed and capsized her, and all who were on board were precipitated into the water. The survivors stated that the French père refused to make for the shore, crying out that his favourite pupil was lost, and that he would perish with him. Whether this is true, or whether the survivors thought that they were a little lax in their efforts to save the Muzungu, and so invented the story to account for his being drowned, I do not know. At any rate, the gentle père found his grave in the mighty lake.

At the beginning of July negotiations were going on between Junker and the Arabs, through Mackay, for the purchase of cloth to send to Emin. Several loads were satisfactorily purchased, and Mwanga

promised permission for them to be sent. During this
time many baptisms took place at night. Samweli came
also several times from his hiding-place, and as an
example of the intelligent way in which the Baganda
people read the Bible, he asked about the many bodies
of the saints which were said to have arisen in connection with the crucifixion. Also he wanted to know
what I made of our Saviour's saying of S. John—"If I
will that he tarry till I come," &c.

We now set to work packing some things for Emin
Pasha and Captain Casati. It was a great pleasure to
Mackay and me to be able to send them a few European articles, along with the cloth which Junker had
purchased. The Tripoli Turk, Mahomet Biri, undertook
the charge of the caravan, which a few weeks later left
Buganda, and successfully accomplished the journey.
This was the first effort made to relieve Emin Pasha.
Mackay a second time sent him a small caravan. For
this and his other services the Khedive of Egypt conferred upon him an Order of the Medij. For an account
of the third and greatest effort to relieve Emin,
by the important expedition which has been led by
Stanley to Kavalli, we may turn to the illustrious
explorer himself, who has a thrilling tale of adventure
and discovery to unfold of this the most interesting
undertaking of modern travel.

Dr. Junker left us on the 14th of July, 1886, taking
with him four of our boys whom we were sending for
safety to the mission station at the south of the lake.

When Dr. Junker was well on his way, Mackay and I determined to ask for leave to take our departure ; and after one or two efforts we were at length admitted to the king's presence. I now come to my last interview with Mwanga. As I said before, Mackay and I had come to the resolution of asking definitely for permission to leave the country, in order that the chiefs might see that we were speaking the truth when we said that if the rulers wished us to go away we were prepared to do so. They had now shown us unmistakably their feeling towards us by the murder of the people whom we taught, and so we determined on this important step.

On the 3rd of August we went to Mengo, and found the king in full "baraza," with all the great earls of the kingdom about him. The king knew what we had come for, and there was an air of general restraint pervading the assembly. Some preliminary business of the kingdom was transacted, and then, at a pause in the proceedings, Mackay went forward, and kneeling at the edge of the king's carpet, and in front of the king—we always sat or knelt, according to native custom, not stood when addressing the king—Mackay began to speak. He asked for canoes that he and I might leave the country. "Why do you want to leave?" asked Mwanga. "We have had nothing but trouble since we have been here," answered Mackay, and, going on, he waxed warmer, saying, "Our place is guarded, our friends interfered with ; " and finally remarked, "Though

I am willing to help you, I am not your slave."
Mackay had always tried to do anything he could in a
friendly way for the king. The last thing which he had
made was a splendid rope out of native fibre. But, so
far from showing gratitude, latterly the king had become
more and more insolent in his demands.

When Mackay said, "I am not your slave," the king
became sarcastic, and the chief judge asked who
guarded our place.

Then the king broke in, "Oh, yes, you have to chop
my firewood, have you not? You have to cook for me.
You are my slave. What is it you wish?"

Mackay replied, "We desire nothing but canoes
that we may go." He then returned to his seat.
The king flatly refused, and then I got up and
knelt down at one side of the king's carpet and
addressed him. Immediately there was an exclama-
tion from the chiefs, "Go in front of the king and
'woza,' plead." I replied, "What is the offence? I
will not plead;" and I, too, returned to my seat.
Then the ordinary business proceeded; but the king
was preoccupied and distrait, and could not hide his
annoyance. Both Mackay and I were surprised at the
change which seemed to have come over the chiefs.
On leaving the presence of the king they showed the
greatest civility to us. One of them carried our camp
stools for us, and the haughty chancellor asked
Mackay to dinner. I went home with Kulugi, and
he was very civil, and said we ought not to mind what

the king said. And when Mackay came back from his
dining out he told me how he had met some of the
great earls and how they apologised for Mwanga's
petulance. Though we had been refused permission
to leave the country, we began to pack up, starting
with the books. We told every one who came near us
that we were going.

A few days later the Arab Said bin Saif's dhow
arrived from Magu, bringing letters, one from the
Consul-General at Zanzibar to Mwanga, and another
from Seyd Burgash, the Sultan of Zanzibar, no doubt
written at the instance of our Consul, who was most
desirous of helping us; but there was no fulcrum on
which to work his lever. British prestige was at a
discount, for the Baganda imagined that Englishmen
might be killed with impunity in Africa. As an
abstract principle, I much question if it is to the
advantage of any great nation to allow its subjects to
be killed without making any inquiry about their
death, even if they be only missionaries. It will be
seen that the Government of our country had encouraged missionary enterprise in Africa, and in the
eyes of the natives, at any rate, had identified itself
with the missionaries by giving them letters of introduction to African chiefs. I know I shall find few
supporters among those interested in missions when I
say that I think it is a mistake, from a political point
of view, for any government to allow its subjects to
penetrate into the interior unless it is prepared to

afford them protection. In case it is not, then, for the sake of its own prestige, it ought to forbid their going.

Under the circumstances no consular letters could be of much value or help to us. We ourselves were far more of a power to be reckoned with than a far-off British Consul, who was writing almost in the dark, since we had much influence with the rising generation, and our following comprised many chiefs, and Christianity was growing every day in power and importance. The rulers found it like a fire; beaten down in one quarter, it sprang up in another with even greater violence.

Mackay and Lourdel read the letters to the king in Kiswahili; and an Arab trader, Said bin Jimè, read the Arabic copy.

The king and chiefs tried to assume an air of indifference, but were evidently listening with interest to the contents of the missive—I need not speak of the letter, for it simply contained polite nothings.

Mackay and I felt that, if we could not both of us get permission to go away, it was necessary that one of us should endeavour to return to England to lay the whole state of the mission before the Committee of the Church Missionary Society at home, and to evoke the sympathy of Christians in England for their suffering and persecuted co-religionists in Africa. It was obviously only right that Mackay should have a change to Europe after his long years in Africa, and so we agreed that he should ask for permission to leave, and tell the king that I would remain.

Mackay started in the morning, taking a present, and had an interview with Mwanga, and told him that he intended to go. " I will never consent to that," said Mwanga, and promised him large gifts of "ensimbè," cowrie shells, and also promised him four milch cows, if he would remain. Afterwards he called him privately, and, when none of the great lords were present, said, twice over, "You shall remain with me, and teach people religion."

When Mackay saw that Mwanga would not consent to his going, he said, "Will you let Bwana Ashe go ?" and, after some parley, the king finally consented to this.

Then came a time of sorrowful farewells. Our house was crowded every evening by faithful friends who came to bid me good-bye. But the saddest leave-taking of all was with Mackay, in whose company I had passed through so many trials and troubles, and who had always proved himself my true, sympathetic, and steadfast friend.

The mission boat had not yet returned from her voyage to the south of the Lake, whither she had gone with Dr. Junker and his party, and so I was obliged to take a passage in the dhow which had come to Buganda a week or two before with the letters, and which was now returning to the further end of the lake. I had a fellow-passenger in an Arab trader whose soubriquet was Khambi Embaya (the bad camp).

He and I parted company a few days later, when I had the good fortune to encounter the little *Eleanor* on her way back to Buganda with letters. I forwarded Mackay's mail by land, and got my party on board the *Eleanor*, and made a quick and prosperous voyage to our port near Musalala.

Khambi Embaya, like so many of my companions, met with a violent death. While I travelled south through Unyamwezi territory, he took the Usukuma road, and he and all his people were killed by the Wasukuma natives a month or two later. The quarrel arose, I believe, because the Arab's slaves wished to draw water for themselves before the natives had watered their own cattle. Angry words arose, blows were struck, the natives collected in force, and in vain the Arab endeavoured to restrain his followers. In the end he and his whole party were annihilated. Some say the quarrel arose because the Arab's people had thrown the corpse of a dead porter into the well which the Wasukuma were using. However it happened, the fact remains that poor Khambi Embaya was killed. It is a sorrowful reflection that the fine qualities which many of these Arabs possess should be prostituted to the shameful and degraded purpose to which they are misapplied in slave-dealing.

My little party consisted of the Wangwana (coast-men), one of whom had a wife whom he had married in Buganda. This woman was a native Muganda, and it seems that she ought not legally to have been removed from the country. At any rate, her friends pursued me for days in order to try and recover her. I knew nothing of this at the time, but supposed that Juma—for that was her husband's name—had acquired her lawfully. Mackay wrote to me afterwards, and told me of the pursuit. The rest of my party was made up of four boys, whom I was taking with the intention of leaving with Gordon at the south of the Nyanza.

And so, as I reclined on the little after-deck of the *Eleanor*, and as the boat glided swiftly onwards, I saw perhaps for the last time the deep rich colouring of the gorgeous panorama which lay stretched before me, while the coast line of Buganda slowly became more dim and undefined in the distance. How peaceful and yet how glorious that living picture appeared in the gold and purple of the setting sun ; but how could there have failed to be a sense of utter sadness in my heart, as I thought of the scenes which had been enacted in that unhappy land of misery and mystery ? How could I fail to call up the familiar faces of the dead—kindly dark faces of faithful friends ; and above all the never-to-be-forgotten, sorrowful, appealing eyes of little Joseph Lugalama.

CHAPTER XX.

A FORTNIGHT'S journey in the *Eleanor* brought me to Bukumbi, the French Mission at the south of the lake, where I landed for a few hours, and was hospitably entertained at dinner by the kindly priests.

Their place was very nice, a regular seminary of young Africans. I could only give a passing glance at their arrangements, which, however, seemed excellent.

It will be interesting to learn hereafter if any of these boys are ordained, and how they bear the yoke of celibacy which the Church of Rome imposes with her orders.

At Bukumbi there was no display of European luxury. In fact, the only costly thing which they seemed to possess was the jewelled cross of their courteous Bishop. Unable as I am to reverence the system which they support, or many of the doctrines which they believe, I can at least reverence the simple devotion of their lives.

On leaving, the Bishop put into my hand a good loaf of bread—a great luxury.

A few more hours and the *Eleanor* was anchored at Muleshi's, the port for Musalala, and at about two o'clock next day I arrived at the Mission, and was warmly welcomed by my old companions, Gordon and Wise, and also not less warmly by the boys whom Mackay and I had sent here for safety. I remained at Musalala two whole days, and then started on my long 800-mile tramp to the coast.

Fourteen days' journey brought me to Uyui, our Mission station, which was at that time occupied by a young Cambridge man, who was a volunteer missionary working at his own charges. He received me kindly, and I spent some days in his house. The day that I arrived news reached us that the Arabs of Unyanyembe intended to waylay and murder a young German trader named Giesiker, and six days later we heard that the attempt on Giesiker's life had been made. The quarrel with Giesiker was not so much that he was a German, but that he was buying ivory and competing with the Arabs in their trade. Hooper, my host, at once sent messengers to Unyanyembe to offer any assistance in his power. Dr. Junker was there at the time, and also the French missionaries, so that we did not think it necessary to go ourselves. The messengers returned, bringing a letter from Brooks, a missionary of the London Missionary Society, who had been one of our companions on the voyage out from England, and who happened at this time to be at Unyanyembe. His letter ran as follows :—

"Tabora,* Sept. 30, 1886.

"DEAR MR. HOOPER,—Your mail-men arrived this morning, and it falls to me to answer your letter and

* Same as Unyanyembe.

kind offer to Mr. Giesiker. I arrived here on Monday
morning, and heard of the serious affair of Giesiker from
the Arabs. I went at once to his camp, and found that
he had been moved to the French Mission, where I saw
him. Poor fellow! he is severely wounded. It appears
that Seyid bin Juma (Liwli or Governor of Unyanyembe) had been told that Giesiker would be killed as
soon as he left Tabora, and on Sunday evening, about
ten o'clock, a man crept into his tent and attempted to
take away the light, when all at once a volley of at
least three guns was fired, killing the man who was
attempting to take the light and who was probably one
of the gang; another, a Mungwana, was also shot through
both thighs. Poor Giesiker was shot through the left
arm a little below the shoulder. Another ball, which is
still in the thigh, passed between the knee and hip-
joint, also left. But the feet are worst of all : the left is
shot away from the ankle-joint, right under the sole,
you could hardly cover it with one hand ; the right is
also as bad, and one ball has passed through the foot.
Poor fellow, I fear very much for his life. He has a
little fever now and again, is also light-headed; still, he
is a strong fellow, and may possibly pull through ; but
it will take from eight to twelve months. I have
started his caravan off with Tipotip, thinking, with
others, that was the best thing to be done. It will
save him much anxiety, and perhaps danger. The
French missionaries are dressing him ; and, should
they run out of medicine, they will come to you or us.
Dr. Junker is well, and left Ituro this morning with

Tipotip. Give my kind regards to Mr. Ashe, and
Stokes when he comes, and not forgetting yourself,
" I remain, yours sincerely,
" A. Brooks."

Brooks himself was murdered three years later, near
Zanzibar.

I found difficulty in collecting porters, so I determined
to travel as lightly as possible, and I obtained four faithful
Zanzibaris, who undertook to make the journey from
Uyui to Zanzibar. I had four small bundles, consisting
of papers and books, blankets, clothing, food, besides a
kettle, a pot, and a gunpowder flask for a water-bottle.
My arms consisted of a light fowling-piece (muzzle-
loading), a small carbine (also muzzle-loading), and a
six-chambered revolver. Also I had a broken Bahuma
spear, which had belonged to Lugalama, and which I
usually carried. The men carried the other weapons.
I used to have the same food as my porters, except that
I had some biscuits and pots of jam which Hooper had
given me. He despised such things; but I could not
swallow " ugali "* without something of the kind to make
it go down. In one of our camps † we had a narrow
escape from fire. We were inside a " boma " (fence) made
of thorn bushes, and were sleeping in straw huts. The
men had lighted a big fire outside the opening of their
hut. I did not think it very safe, but while I was

---

* Coarse native porridge.

† This was an old camp containing vast numbers of small straw
huts which had been made by the porters of some other larger
caravan.

reflecting about it I dozed off. I had been ill at Uyui,
and had not yet recovered. I was suddenly awakened
fully by seeing a blaze of fire all about me. Instantly
I jumped up and seized one or two things, and made
for the opening in the boma. It was closed with a
thorny bush, which I could not remove. Mwalimu
one of my men, came and pulled it away, and I got
out; but my few belongings were still in the boma.
The men had just time to snatch up some of them and
run. I had run out without my boots, and I felt terribly
afraid that I should lose them. However, the men had
thoughtfully rescued them. By this time the whole
great camp was on fire, and we found ourselves again
within a circle of advancing flame. Again there was
a stampede, and we got the things some little distance
from the burning huts. When I counted my losses, I
found that most of my books and papers had been
burnt, and also a dressed antelope skin, which I had
obtained from the brave young martyr, Mukassa or
Musa. Lugalama's spear was saved. All the food of
my men had been burnt; and though we were still far
in the Uyui wilderness, they said, "Do not be troubled,
we are black men, and can go without food for a day
or two without much inconvenience." Though their
own rice was burnt, they had saved my biscuit, so
when we halted I gave them some biscuits and coffee,
and the next evening we reached Itura, on the far side
of the "terrible garden," the Mugunda Mukali. I was
very unwell here, and could hardly crawl through the
great wilderness. However, after two or three days'

journey through the scrubby forest, we came on an Arab caravan going to Unyanyembe. The Arabs visited me, and I told them I wanted to buy a donkey which they had with them. The owner of the donkey had only lately come from Muscat, and did not know whether a bill from me was worth having. However, his friend assured him that I was an Englishman and that it would be all right. So in an African wilderness, 500 miles from Zanzibar, this stranger Arab handed over to me a fine Muscat donkey with saddle and trappings in exchange for a dirty piece of paper, with an order written in English for 110 dollars. It was a heavy price, but I seldom, I think, have made a better bargain than the splendid little animal, which proved a godsend to me on my journey. I have mentioned this incident, as I think it shows that Englishmen had gained credit from the Arabs for being, at any rate, honourable in their dealings. I had no tent, and none of the usual paraphernalia of travellers on this journey; but I suffered very little from fever, and though I used to encamp without any "boma," in the wildest spots, I never was troubled by any prowling wild beasts. We always kept fires burning during the night.

In due course I reached Mpwapwa, where my friends, the Coles, most kindly received me, and it was here I first saw Dr. Pruen, whom I was to meet again on my second return journey from the Nyanza, and in company with him and his courageous wife to pass through the insurgents to Zanzibar.

After leaving these kind friends I was once more on

my way, passing again the glorious Mamboya mountains, where I was hospitably entertained by an old
friend, Roscoe, at that time in charge of the mission
station. Six days' march from here brought me to
Mkange, where I saw again the ocean. One in my
case can enter into the feelings of the retreating
ten thousand when they once more beheld the sea,
which, in their case at least, was aptly called Euxine,
and broke out with the glad cry of "Thalatta!
Thalatta!" (The sea! The sea!) I reached Sadaani
on a Sunday, and proceeded at once to buy oranges
and a mango without the faintest pang of conscience,
for I did not recollect the fact that it was Sunday
till after I had finished my meal. Whether or not
I should have abstained from the purchase had I
known the day, it is needless to enquire. In the New
Year of 1887 I saw the white cliffs of Dover once more,
and on landing in London I went straight to the rooms
of an old college friend, Rev. Robert Walker, of whose
subsequent experiences I shall have something to tell
in another chapter.

It may be of interest to state the first thing which
struck me as strange in civilized England after returning
from the heart of Africa was to find moral sentiments
displayed in the omnibuses, which, however, a little
study showed me were only advertisements of soap.
When my friend received me I had no idea that in a
little more than six months I should be setting out
with him on a second journey to the Dark Continent.
But so it was to be.

CHAPTER XXI.

It is needless to trouble the patient reader with another account of a journey to the Nyanza. Walker and I had a small and compact caravan of about eighty men. We had also riding donkeys, which greatly lightened the weariness of the march. The same, to me, familiar scenes were passed, but the journey was free from many of the hardships of the first undertaking. The blue hills of Mamboya were reached. The kindly hospitality of the Coles at Kisokwe was once more enjoyed; the bitter water wilderness was traversed; the Wagogo warriors again appeared in due order, and were again left far behind as we still held on our way through the "terrible garden." But we did not go by way of Uyui, where the chief had become hostile, but passing out of the Muganda Mukali we struck further east to Ikungu, and from there through another long wilderness, with low hills on our left and wide bare illimitable grassy plains on our right, stretching away into the Watatura country till we came out of this wilderness near our friend Mutinginya. Passing Tambalali and Sungwezi and Nyawa, we reached the chief's village at Usongo. At one of the villages we received a gift of a fine young ram. One of our men tied a cord to him and tried to lead him, but he refused to budge; so the man dragged him by main force, resisting at every step. The happy thought struck me of harnessing the donkey to him, which we did, and so willy-nilly he had to go; however, he lay down and suffered himself to be dragged. This was too cruel a proceeding, so we had to stop and butcher him; there was no little intercessor here, so he lost his life. It is useful to know that sheep will not travel, though goats are easily led. Just before we entered the last wilderness before Usongo, Walker and I suddenly saw an apparition, of the leanest boy we had ever beheld, walking with our men. On making inquiries who or what the poor skeleton was, we found that he was a slave who had been raided by the Arabs from Lubemba; they had treated him cruelly, having hacked off one or two of his fingers and burned him frightfully for some small offence. They had left him to die of small-pox at Itura. However, Songoro, for that was his name, managed to pull through, and took refuge with us. No one came to claim him, so we let him come on with us. He had plenty to eat, and held the desirable post of cook's assistant. I afterwards brought him to Zanzibar with me; but by that time he was the fattest of the party. The consul gave me a paper of freedom for him, so that his former cruel owner could not claim him again.

We now took a more easterly route than the one

which I had followed on the former journey, and
passed through the naked Wasukuma, who were exceedingly turbulent and troublesome, especially about
letting us draw water. These were the people who had
killed my former Arab travelling companion, Kambi
Embaya, owing to a quarrel about water.

Bishop Parker, and Blackburn, whom I mentioned as
one of the members of the former expedition, had preceded us to the Nyanza, and we all met at the south of
the lake at Busambiro, where Mackay had arrived some
months before from Buganda with a large quantity of
valuable property. A strong letter which Consul Holm-
wood had written from Zanzibar to Mwanga seems to have
really frightened the foolish tyrant, who had allowed
Mackay to leave. Thus the great controversy between
Mwanga and Mackay was settled by Mwanga's consent-
ing to Mackay's departure. The latter, however, had no
idea when he left of abandoning the mission, so when he
reached Musalala, where Gordon and Wise still were stationed, he represented the matter to them, and Gordon
offered to go alone and place himself in the power of the
young autocrat. Mackay had previously begged of the
king to receive another missionary in his stead, and
Mwanga had accordingly sent a " mubaka," messenger, to
invite Gordon and to bring him in safety to the capital.
The mission at Musalala, like that at Uyui, had been
abandoned owing to the rapacity of the Wanyamwezi
chiefs, who had become more insolent and importunate
in their demands for cloth and other presents, and was

now in the territory of Roma at Mutereza, near the village of the sub-chief Makolo, whose people were a sort of mixture of Bazinja and Wanyamwezi. We were therefore in territory which was completely under the power of Mwanga, whose warriors some few years before had raided Roma and sent him flying for his life, so that Roma now looked on Mwanga as the greatest monarch on earth. We reached the Nyanza in a time of pouring·rain, and there were no houses and no proper place of shelter; although Mackay had been indefatigable, and had begun to build a long low substantial house, something like a native "tembe" only larger, but, like the tembe, it had a mud roof. At Mutereza, under Bishop Parker as president, six of us held a missionary conference, and we wrote a letter to King Mwanga in the new Bishop's name, in which, though we referred to the death of Hannington, we yet explained that we were people of peace, and that we only wished to enter his country and live there in a friendly way. This letter was duly despatched and presented by Gordon; it gave no little offence, and the king covered it with ashes, a sign of a war challenge. However, Kolugi, whom I have before mentioned, scattered them on the ground, as he saw that Gordon did not understand the action, and advised him to take no notice of the matter. In a month or two the boat returned to the south of the lake with a messenger, who was sent, not to the Bishop, but to Mackay. The messenger was instructed to return bringing on the new "Muzungu" (white man) who had arrived at Musalala with me, namely Walker, but Mwanga sent no message to me of any kind. At the same time Gordon wrote strongly urging that some one else should be sent to join him. After long consideration we decided to accede to Mwanga's request for the new "Muzungu," and so Walker, like Gordon, quite understanding the kind of host by whom he was to be entertained, was perfectly willing to proceed to Buganda. But before he left he was to have his first experience of the dark side of African life. My old companion in travel, Blackburn, had made a journey, with the view of helping Hooper, (formerly at Uyui) to open a new mission station at Nassa on Speke Gulf. Both of them suffered much from fever, and Blackburn therefore returned to Mutereza. He did not seem well, but we did not think that anything very serious was the matter. Two days later he took to his bed. At this time we were all living in huts, except the Bishop, who preferred his tent. Blackburn rapidly grew worse, and the rest of us watched by him in turns night and day, while his servant Zaburi tended him most faithfully; the end came suddenly, and was a great shock to us, since he seemed decidedly better a day or two before he died. Late on the tenth day after he took to his bed the Bishop called me, and I just reached his side in time to see him breathe his last. One of the porters in our caravan had died shortly before, and the chiefs and people said that it was "mwiko" or forbidden to bury him, since he had died

of dysentery, so we were obliged to wrap the corpse up
and have it carried away and thrown into the swamp.
We feared they might make some similar objection to
to our burying our missionary friend, and so we called
our men and had the grave dug at once. It was a time
of great sorrow to us, and deeply we felt for Blackburn's
young wife whom he had left, with a noble devotion to
duty, although he himself was in no fit condition to return
to his work. She had hoped to join him at some station
near the coast, and indeed had all her preparations
made for the journey when the sorrowful tidings of
her husband's death reached her.

Whatever may be said against missionaries and their
lack of zeal or their want of faithfulness to duty, there are
not a few unknown graves in Eastern Africa which are a
proof that, though some may have been unworthy, there
are many of all denominations who, like Blackburn, have
put duty before even life, and have bravely died at
their posts.

Our party was now reduced to four, and a deep sense
of sadness had come over us. It was arranged that the
Bishop should go and join Hooper and his companion
Deekes who had meantime arrived, at Nassa, and that
Walker should, according to the arrangement previously
made, proceed to Buganda. A few months before this
I had decided to return to Zanzibar, and had signified
this intention to the Bishop; but he and my other
companions were anxious that I should wait some
time longer, and I had acceded to their request. The

last few days had been spent in making preparations for the start of our friends, and the Sunday before Easter we had our last communion together. The Bishop seemed in very good spirits and fairly well, but he had suffered much from fever, and the attacks seemed to be more frequent. On Sunday night, 25th of March, he left us as usual. However, towards morning he was seized with what appeared to be a violent attack of ague. Mackay got a hot-water bottle and put it to his feet, and we wrapped him up well in blankets ; he seemed better, and we called his boy who remained with him. We thought that it was only an ordinary fever. Next morning, however, the Bishop got up and and wandered out, and Walker met him and saw that he looked like a man walking in his sleep; he helped him back to bed, and we watched by him. In the afternoon he became terribly delirious, and Walker, who was alone with him, had to call for more help, and so two of us stayed by his side. Towards evening he grew calmer and seemed to have sunk into a troubled sleep. We arranged to remain with him by turns during the night. So Walker and I went to bed early, leaving Mackay to take the first watch. I had not been gone long when I heard some one calling me—it was one of the Bishop's black boys. As I hurriedly threw on my clothes the thought of the last summons I had received to the bedside of a sick companion stole across my mind, and with much misgiving I hastened to the bishop's room. He was now in the house which

s

Mackay had nearly finished, and I was shocked to see that death was written unmistakeably on his face.

Mackay had just hurried out to get some chartreuse, in hope of staving off the collapse. The Bishop was faintly breathing when I reached him, but in another moment all was over.

The bitter weeping of the faithful boy who had been watching by his master, showed me that he too had realised the sad truth. Mackay now returned and saw that another of our little band had passed away, and Walker came in at the same time, so with silent sorrow and awe we three stood and looked at the calm still face and tried to understand that the head of the mission had been taken from us. It was a pouring wet night, but it was necessary to have the grave made at once. So the Bishop's Christian porters, who had accompanied him from Freretown, were summoned to prepare their master's resting-place beside that of Blackburn. There was no time to make a coffin, but reverently we wrapped the dead in some of the beautiful bark cloths which Mackay had obtained from Buganda, and just as the first faint streak of dawn appeared in the eastern sky, we laid him in the grave. Mackay read part of the burial service in Swahili, that the Bishop's porters might understand; and as we turned sadly away, the morning song of the birds might well have seemed to be a voice from Heaven, echoing the glorious words which had been sounding in our ears :—" Blessed are the dead which die in the Lord :

even so saith the Spirit; for they rest from their labours."

A few days later and we had said farewell to Walker who left on the 1st of April in the mission-boat for Buganda. Of his grand reception there by King Mwanga I need say little, except that it somewhat resembled my own, which I have already described, only it was still more imposing, and Mwanga even rose up to meet his guest—a mark of high honour. Walker, during his brief sojourn in the country, on the whole seems to have formed a fairly favourable opinion of this young king; but Mwanga's misgovernment, his raids upon his own people, his licentious behaviour and his tyranny, became so intolerable to the Baganda that . they determined to depose him.

Mwanga's monthly progresses into the provinces, his seizing the wives and daughters and cattle of his subjects, left him without a single supporter among the mass of his people; and the clever young chiefs, who were mostly reformers or readers of the Moslem and Christian faiths, became for once united and easily deposed him. And it seems that the old saying, "Whom the gods wish to destroy they first make mad," was true in Mwanga's case, for he relinquished the wise policy of attempting to play off one party against another, and to his ruin actually threw them into one another's arms. He would not admit as a factor in his policy the belief of the reformers in God, which clashed with his belief in

himself. The haughty Moslems called the royal cows
killed by the uncircumcised, defiled, and spurned the
unholy flesh, while the Christians quietly kept away
from work on Sundays. Who is this God who must be
honoured before kings? So Mwanga decreed that God
must go and the worshippers of God must be swept for
ever from his path. The summons went forth for " all
Buganda " to come and enlarge the royal pond—Nyanza
(sea) it was called out of flattery, because it was the
king's ; but Mwanga will make it a Nyanza indeed. So
all the chiefs are called to the work. The young king
arms his favourites with Snider rifles, and some have
even Winchester repeaters. A body-guard truly, but
more ornamental than useful. He comes down to see
the work with his boys. One is insolently set over the
chiefs. Mwanga will have no one armed but his own
immediate followers, and commands the workers to
come unarmed. But they come armed, nominally for the
protection of the king, really to intimidate him ; and so
he must get rid of them. Pokino and the chancellor,
who hated and despised the foreign religions, with
other old chiefs, wished to return to the palmy days of
the cruel Suna. The country was going to the dogs.
Slaves and the young were beginning to have opinions,
and dangerous doctrines of the most radical description
were gradually undermining the old ideas, and every
day gaining ground. Desperate diseases require desperate
remedies. Mutesa had crushed Islam out and drenched
it out in blood. True it had grown up again, but this

time it shall not. Mukasa, the mighty god of the
Nyanza, shall give his help, and shall be honoured by
such a holocaust of victims in the slain believers in
Allah and Katonda as has never before been heard of
in the annals of Buganda.

The bloody Mujasi, head of "the Bajasi" body-guard,
a bitter Moslem, is not consulted. Could he not have
been used as the tool to carry out the slaughter of the
Christian "Basalo Salo" body-guard, and then be
broken and cast away? Sanity would answer yes, but
madness, shrieking no, will sweep to a speedier revenge.
All shall perish together, all shall be packed into canoes,
landed on a distant island in the lake, and left to a slow
and miserable death.

The day comes; the two great body-guards of
Christians and Moslems are marched down to the
Nyanza under their chiefs, while his personal guard of
useless and insolent boys accompanies the king. The
Moslems and Christians are ordered on board. Mujasi is
ill and cannot go. The Christians refuse to embark
unless with the king. Mwanga, with a heart full of apprehension and bitterness, baffled and angry, hastens back to
his capital, where the old fox Pokino and the chancellor
are waiting to hear of the success of the scheme. The
only news is the ugly word flung out, " bajemye,"—they
have rebelled.

To-morrow the rebels will arrive. To-day is "Sabiti,"
Sunday. But there will be work to-morrow—and the

morrow comes. Mujasi the murderer, before he meets his own bloody death, must first be the instrument used to hurl Mwanga from his throne. He comes one way with his following, and the Christian guards another. The Crescent and the Cross close in on heathendom; heathendom, as usual, fights but feebly, and flies. Mwanga, with his boy bodyguard and a number of women, is soon hurrying away from the scene of his former glories, to seek a refuge on the lake. He is followed, but scornfully allowed to go his way. Mujasi has brought Kiwewa, a quiet man, Mutesa's eldest son. And Kiwewa duly "eats Buganda." Thus the bloodless revolution is accomplished.

European missionaries and Moslem missionaries, *i.e.* Arab slave traders, are called into the royal presence—freedom of trade and toleration of all religions is granted. Kagwa Apolo, formerly gashed and beaten by Mwanga, was elevated to the "bakungu" or peerage, and became Mukwenda, Earl of Singo, while Nyonyi Entono (the small bird), who had been mutilated by Mwanga, was given the highest post in the kingdom, and was now Katikiro or Lord High Chancellor of Buganda. Samweli, the faithful bringer-in of tribute, was made head storekeeper. Zakariya Kizito, whose letter to me I give in the appendix, also received a high office; while Mujasi was made Kangao, Earl of Bulemezi. Mwanga meanwhile had reached the lake, and had obtained from the old chief Jumba five canoes, into which he crowded his people; but I subjoin Mackay's graphic account of the young king's flight:—

"*Usambiro, Kwa Makolo,*
"*Oct.* 23*rd,* 1888.

"Mwanga is at present at Magu, having reached that place with only one canoe and six women, and between thirty and forty boys.

"When I heard the news, I at once sent two of my most trustworthy servants to Magu, directing them to try and fetch the poor fugitive king away by night, as I feared the Arabs would betray him. I know it is a great risk to have anything to do in the way of trying to save him from being taken back a prisoner to Buganda, where he will surely be put to death, as another king is on the throne. Murderer and persecutor as he has been, I yet have not the faintest doubt but that it becomes us to do everything in our power to return him good for evil. My men reached him, and found him eager to jump at my offer, but unable to come away from the Arabs' clutches, fearing they would send after him and arrest him. He sent back here, with my men, two of his lads, begging me to go to Magu myself and endeavour to get him out of there, suggesting that one of the brethren at Nassa should come here to take my place while I conducted him (Mwanga) to the coast.

"Anticipating such a desire on his part, I had previously sent to Nassa, asking Deekes to come over here for a month. Possibly he may come, but can scarcely be here for several days yet. It will be no easy matter,

but I am willing to take the poor creature as far as
Usongo, where I can give him in charge of Stokes.

"From the two boys sent here by Mwanga, I have
learnt the whole story of the rebellion in Buganda, and
Mwanga's perilous flight to Magu.

"It appears that the king was aware for some time
that his subjects meant to rebel. He learned this
plainly on a trip he took recently to the border of
Bunyoro, when some of his chiefs refused to obey
orders. On returning to the capital he went on a
boating excursion to Ntebe (at the mouth of Murchison
Bay). His body-guard refused to accompany him back
in the canoes, so he returned to his capital (Mengo)
with only his pages. Next day he ordered the drums
to beat for a public audience, but no one appeared.
For a couple of days his enclosures were deserted, and
after that, he heard that the Katikiro and chiefs had
elected his younger brother (named Kayondo) king.
By-and-by troops appeared at Mwanga's gates, so he
gathered all his thousand women, and with the little
boys about him (some two score or more) whom he
armed with Snider rifles, which he had just purchased
from Stokes's agent, made a dash by a back way
to Munyonyo, on the creek. Only a few canoes were
there. These he filled with as many of the women
and boys as he could, and set off. Soon, however,
all the canoes, except the one the king was in,
deserted, and Mwanga had to coast all the way to Magu
with only one canoe, paddled by his boys, he himself

helping. He managed to get one fisherman from Sesse
to steer. This man had once been as far as Kageye.
Had Mwanga not got this man's aid, he never could
have fetched this side of the lake. He was recognised
at one or two places, where he had to put ashore for
food, and had to fight his way to get afloat again. The
only person of position who accompanied him was
Kawuta, nominally head-cook, but a powerful chief.
He, too, deserted after reaching Magu, but had to
return there, as the canoe in which he tried to go
back to Buganda was nearly swamped. Mwanga then
gave Kawuta permission to go back with a few of the
boys, in a small vessel belonging to a coast trader. By
Kawuta he sent a letter to the Katikiro (written, of
course, by the Arabs), begging to be sent for to Buganda.
This he had done just before he got my message, otherwise he says he would not have requested the Arabs to
send a letter. At present he has six women and thirty
more boys with him. At first the Arabs treated him
hospitably, but now are fleecing him of most of his
Snider rifles for clothing and food. He is already
heartily sick of his position in their hands, and wishes
to get to the coast. Hence his sending to me an
imploring message, begging me to come in person to
Magu and take him anywhere I like, or slay him if I
will! He will go with me to Europe if I will take
him, for he has heard that the Emperor of the French
found an asylum in England after being vanquished by
Germany.

" I only hope that, like Nebuchadnezzar, he will get
understanding to ' know that the Most High ruleth in
the kingdom of men, and giveth it to whomsoever He
will.' May his present affliction bring him to his
knees, and teach him to break off his sins by righteousness ! . . . ."

I may here take leave of Mwanga, where he appears
at his best, helping in the canoe and fighting his way
back to his boats like a man, and winning his way to
Magu.

To return now to Buganda. The revolution was
effected without bloodshed, and Mwanga's frightful
tyranny passed away like an unsubstantial dream.
And a time of marvellous peace dawned on the unhappy
kingdom ; but it was only like a burst of sunlight in
a stormy sky, and soon new troubles arose. The
Christians had obtained the lion's share of the power
and influence because they were the more powerful
party, while the new Kangao Mujasi and his following
viewed with ill-concealed envy the good fortune of
their opponents. This did not escape the notice of the
Arab slave traders, who formed a plot with Mujasi to
murder the Christian chiefs as they came from the
king's reception. The plot proved a complete success.
Mujasi, aided by the Arabs, opened a murderous volley
on the Christian chiefs, as they streamed out from the
king's presence. Young Gabunga, the admiral, my
faithful friend, was shot dead ; others also fell, a scene
of wild confusion ensued, the Christians had not time

to gather in force and were driven away. They left
the capital in a compact body, and a new distribution
of chieftainships took place. Mujasi now became
Mukwenda, Earl of Singo. Bugalla, whose story I have
told on p. 129, became Kymbugwe, or keeper of the
palace. The Cross had now yielded for a time before
the Crescent, and the triumphant Moslems determined
to drive the missionaries, both English and French,
out of the country. Walker, Gordon, and Monseigneur Lavinhàc, Pères Lourdel and Denoit, and
a lay brother—six Europeans in all—were summoned
into the presence of the chiefs. The priests had received
some warning of what they might expect, and had
come provided with a few necessaries, such as food and
blankets carried by some boys. Walker and Gordon,
however, went just as they were. On reaching
Bugala's enclosure they were seized and thrust into a
dirty hut, strongly guarded, where they were kept seven
days. The mission-houses were meanwhile sacked, and
everything they contained was either stolen or destroyed.
On the eighth day the prisoners were marched down
to the lake and allowed to go on board the mission-
boat with a number of their boys. The Frenchmen
were allowed to take some loads of cowrie shells and
about twenty persons, mostly boys, with them. They
generously shared all their things with their English
brothers in adversity. And so this strange party found
a fitting refuge together in the " Eleanor " or Mirembe,
which was her native name, the word " mirembe " mean-

ing peace. Walker was robbed of his coat and hat, and
even his trousers, before being allowed to start on the
long and perilous voyage. One of the kindly Frenchmen, however, gave him a pair of corduroy trousers and
a blanket, and with one of their party thus arrayed, they
pushed off into the lake with light hearts and a sense
of the joy of freedom after their wearisome imprisonment. But their adventures were not yet over. I
cannot forbear giving Walker's account of the circumstances of their shipwreck later on. He says :—

"After rowing for some hours, and being well out of
sight of the starting-place, we determined to go to some
island and cook food, and arrange the boat better. We
landed, made fires, cooked rice and wheat. A heavy
shower came on, and most of us were rather damp. It
was a nice island with hippopotamuses playing about
in the water near shore. At sunset we went to the
boat and began to row ; we had not gone far when a
cry was raised of " kiboko " (hippo). We had gone on
to the top of one of them. A rush of water showed us
that we had a hole in the bottom of the boat. Gordon
told the men to bail the water out. I repeated the
remark. The bishop (Lavinhàc) came to me and said
something about dying. I was getting over the rail at
the side of the boat, so as to be more free in case of its
sinking. I got off the boat and sat in the water, and
the boat turned over away from the place where I was
swimming. I made for the shore, about 150 yards
off. As I looked back I saw the captain, many of the

sailors, Gordon, and two of the Frenchmen, following me. All the rest were struggling in the water. I saw the boat was still floating on its side (not quite wrong way up), and that many had scrambled on to it. I gained the shore, and was able to give a hand over the rough stones to the much exhausted Père Lourdel, who had no boots on. In course of time Gordon and the bishop came ashore and all the sailors. One Zanzibar man who was unable to swim, the other two Frenchmen and a crowd of boys and girls were drifting nearer to the shore on the inverted boat. Every moment I expected the boat would disappear. A drum came ashore, which I beat vigorously. A canoe appeared at a distance, but would not come near. The captain and other sailors then swam to the wreck and brought off some of the smaller children. Another canoe appeared and came to where I stood beating the drum, the man took the sticks from me and gave his peculiar call for help ; soon another canoe came on the scene, and one by one the canoes brought the people ashore. Five of the Frenchmen's men were missing. It was sad to think that five of our companions in trouble were lost."

They managed at length, with the generous help of some natives, to get the boat ashore, and then came the question of repairing her. He goes on :—

" The fourth of the Frenchmen is a sort of cook or carpenter. He looked at the boat and said it could be mended, but when he found there were no tools he gave up the job. I therefore undertook to patch the boat with the spokeshave. I chopped a piece of board in two, which I got out of the bottom of the boat; one piece I fixed, with the captain's help, inside the boat over the larger hole, and fastened the ends down with wedges driven under the ribs. Then we got some rope and pulled it to pieces. Most fortunately the Frenchmen had a pail of dripping; this we worked up into the tow and drove it in all round and under our board. Then we filled up the hole with large pads of this tow and dripping from the outside, and nailed and screwed pieces of board over them. The leeches in the water bit my legs. At about midday of the third day at the island, the boat was pronounced to be ready for sea. I confess I felt bad as we rowed away from shore. Miles away from land, thirty-four souls on board, and only a pad of tow and dripping to keep the water out. The good hand of the Lord was upon us; we came on slowly day by day, buying food with the Frenchmen's shells, sleeping in grass-built huts at night, or on the sandy shore by large fires. What was wetted by the rain was soon dried by the sun. After seventeen days we came to the Frenchmen's house at midnight (at Bukumbi). They gave us a good supper and bed, and the next day, at 5 P.M., we arrived at Mackay's."

Here I must leave these brave adventurers to rest after their perilous voyage, and return once more to Buganda, where another revolution soon took place. I give the account of it in Mackay's own words; the news was brought to him by a dozen of our former pupils, who had effected their escape from Buganda in a canoe. He writes as follows :—

"It appears that soon after the departure of our brethren from Buganda, the authorities expressed their regret at having allowed the white men to go in safety, as it was feared they would join Mwanga on this side (*i.e.* south of Nyanza at Magu), and aided by the Christian chiefs who had fled (although in another direction), return and fight Kiwewa. Poor Kiwewa was not, however, long allowed to enjoy his exaltation to the throne. His head chiefs, who called themselves Moham-medans, in company with the Arabs, sorely pressed the king to be circumcised. Meantime the king was being advised by the old Katikiro (chancellor), then retired and living near the sepulchre of Mutesa, not to yield to the demand of the Arab party, as his father Mutesa had not been circumcised. Kiwewa therefore determined to try and rid himself of his new Katikiro, Kimbugwe (Bugala) and Mukwenda (formerly Mujasi), and others who were pressing him to yield to their request that he should become a pronounced Mussulman. The king tried to poison them, but the scheme failed. Next he ordered their attendance one day at a private audience, when he said he would consent to be circumcised. At this audience the king's executioners suddenly seized the Katikiro, Kimbugwe, and Mukwenda (Mujasi) ; Kiwewa seizing a spear and killing the two last ; but as he

was about to slay his chief minister, a gun was fired
at him by a lad of the Katikiro's, whereupon the
king fled, and the chief minister got himself released.
The Katikiro at once selected another prince, named
Kalema, one of Mutesa's eldest sons, who some years
ago murdered his brother Ma'anda, and calling the Arabs
to his aid, circumcised him and set him on the throne
now vacated by Kiwewa. The latter fled to Nabulagala
and took refuge at the grave of his father. The Arabs,
however, attacked that place and drove him from it,
plundering and burning the houses of the old Katikiro,
in the hope probably of trying to recover their debts.
Meantime they act as Kalema's body-guard, while
Kiwewa has fled to Singo, the part of Buganda nearest
Bunyoro, and has there been joined by the old Katikiro,
Kolugi, and many others who were Mwanga's principal
chiefs. I believe that Kiwewa has sent to recall the
the Christian chiefs and soldiers, who had fled to
Busàgara and Bunyoro; and should these consent to
come to his aid, we may soon hear of the overthrow of
Kalema and his Arab guard, and the re-establishment
of Kiwewa on the throne. These events, coupled with
the difficulties on Lake Nyassa, on the Upper Congo,
and on the Nile, render the question now paramount,
*Is Arab or European influence henceforth to prevail in
Central Africa?* The answer to this question rests with
Christian Europe. God grant that the suicidal policy
of ABANDON, adopted in the Soudan, may not now be
followed in East Africa."

The sequel to the story is certainly no less astonishing and tragic than its beginning. Kiwewa was eventually captured, and was poisoned, and Kalema succeeded in establishing himself in the kingdom. But, at the instigation of his fanatical Arab supporters, he ordered the universal imposition of the rite which Kiwewa had killed Mujasi and Bugalla for attempting to force upon him. The violence and bloodshed which the attempt to compel the acceptance of this new edict occasioned, filled the minds of the people with fear and disgust, and very soon the defeated Christians, who had withdrawn in a compact body to the neighbouring kingdom of Busagala, were joined by a daily growing mass of their disaffected countrymen.

There was, as might be expected, little real unity between the two opposing parties of Christians, the people of the Pope and the people of the Book, and constant quarrelling and bickering took place. Well was it for the cause that there were such as Samwili, the faithful bringer of tribute, and the solid Sembera, called Mackay, on the Protestant side; or the gentle and gallant young generalissimo, Nyonyi Entono, to represent the Roman Catholic interest. So that actual fighting, at any rate, was staved off. But, besides these theological differences, a new and grave difficulty arose in the vast influx of strangers, who claimed the hospitality of the King of Busagala. But, though Entarè could receive hundreds, when the host of his Baganda guests swelled to thousands it became a most serious

T

matter, and the visitors had to make cattle raids on the neighbouring Banaruanda to keep themselves in food and favour.

Meanwhile Kalema had collected an army, which he sent to punish Mukotanyi, the new King of the Baziba, who had supplied the fugitive Baganda with canoes in which to cross the Katonga. And the Christian leaders, hearing of the plight of their friend, marched with all their following to his aid. A battle was fought, and Kalema's force was utterly routed, and the victorious Christians advanced into Budu, one of the provinces of Buganda. Kalema killed his defeated general when that unfortunate officer returned to the capital, and sent a new army, under a fresh commander, to meet the approaching Christian force. At the first onset, Kalema's host was driven back, and many of the leaders killed, among whom were the renegade one-eyed Arab, Masudi—present at Bishop Hannington's capture— Serokoto, who murdered my boy friend, the young Admiral Gabunga, and Kyambalango, the former Governor of Budu and prime favourite of Mutesa, who played a prominent part in Buganda politics. This was the splendid-looking chief whom, on my first intro- duction to him, I mistook for Mutesa. Kyambalango was wounded, and, making his escape from the battle- field, took refuge in a hut. He was followed, and his pursuers surrounded the house and set fire to it, and soon all that was mortal of him perished in the flames.

But Kalema's army, though repulsed was not routed,

and they rallied, knowing that to return to Kalema meant death, so that they fought with the courage of despair. And soon a terrible disaster overtook the Christian host in the death of its brave young general, Nyonyi Entono.* Disheartened by the death of their leader, discouraged and disunited, the Christians then retreated, as best they could, to Busagala. Samweli of the tribute, in writing of this battle, tells also of the death of Dungu, named Antony, and of the boy Samweli, the same boy of whose baptism I have told the story on page 227. Dungu was a freed man of Samweli's father, and the two were friends. The boy's death is recorded in touching words :—" Also Samweli, our boy, is dead; a compassionate man would not have been able to kill him; but the followers of Islam have no pity; they have killed him."

But King Kalema, besides his fear of enemies without, stood in constant terror of traitors nearer home; and foremost among these was the former chancellor, the old Katikiro. This clever courtier and subtle time-server had managed up to the present, not only to keep his head on his shoulders, but, what was even more surprising, to remain in possession of a considerable part of his ill-gotten wealth. He was, however, more than suspected of treasonable intentions; and it is little wonder that he should ill brook to see those

---

* He was succeeded in the leadership by Kagwa Apollo, a protestant, the hero of the subsequent victory over Kalema and the Arabs.

obsequious Arabs, who formerly had fawned at his own feet, now lording it as the king's chief agents and advisers, while he himself was kept altogether in the background. A conspiracy against Kalema did not appear to promise very much danger, and he might well hope that his old good fortune would still befriend him, and that the tottering power of Kalema would be still less able to resist a revolution than the more stable government of Kiwewa or Mwanga. He was more than a match for the Arabs in cunning; and if he could but hold on for a few more months, he had every prospect of returning once more to place and power. But it was not to be, and his time is come. Though the finger of doom has moved slowly along the dial, it reaches at last the inevitable hour.

Kalema holds a secret baraza, similar to many a one at which the old Katikiro himself had assisted as chief adviser, and whereat he had counselled the death of others far more righteous than himself—Bishop Hannington, Bali ku dembe, our boys, and many an unrecorded name—and now it is his own name that is whispered about among those bowed-down heads, and his own destruction that is being compassed.

His sentence is passed, and soon carried out; his houses are surrounded by a howling mob, and stripped of every valuable, and he himself, hemmed in on all sides, dies at last like an old lion, burnt to death in his own blazing house. Thus perished and came to a fearful end the most polished, ablest, and worst of

Buganda chieftains—according to Emin Pasha the one gentleman in Uganda.

Kalema now saw clearly what would be the policy of any of his disaffected subjects, namely, to possess themselves of the person of one of the royal princes or princesses, the latter especially; for was it not said, as regarded the Christians, they wished to be ruled by a woman, as their co-religionists were ruled by the queen in Bulaya? Hence he came to the fiendish resolution of putting to death every living soul in whose veins ran the royal blood; though it must include even his own children, he will not and does not shrink from it; and so, huddled together in their own houses, the royalty of a great nation is slowly roasted to death. The great number of victims makes the crime more appalling; and yet, in spite of this wholesale massacre, as if some higher power were mocking his bloodthirsty ferocity, the very next news which the miserable fratricide hears is that Mwanga, the only prince whom he has not murdered, and whom he believed to be hundreds of miles away a prisoner in the hands of his enemies, is actually now at his very gates at the head of a large and powerful following, armed with hundreds of guns, and backed by the influence and support of the white men.

But how had Mwanga regained liberty and power? The story is soon told. He succeeded in getting away from the Arabs, and took up his abode with the French priests at Ukumbi. While there he was baptised—let us hope converted also, and hearing that the Christians, who had taken refuge in Busagala, were prepared to help him if he would put himself at their head, he prevailed upon Stokes, now become a trader, to take him to Dumo, near the Kagera river, in the latter's boat. Stokes supplied him with arms and ammunition, and the priests also supplied him with guns, and gave their sanction to the expedition. Mackay and his fellow missionaries, on the other hand, deprecated and discouraged the undertaking.

However, Mwanga, as we have seen, reached Buganda, and soon mustered several thousand followers, mostly armed with spear and shield, though they had 1,100 guns among them. Kalema despatched an army to meet them vastly superior in numbers, and a battle ensued, in which Mwanga's troops were defeated, and his general, Mwemba, killed. Mwanga himself escaped on board Stokes's boat, and made for the Sesse Islands, where he was followed by some 200 of his adherents in canoes. The Sesse people welcomed him eagerly. They form the maritime part and power of Buganda, being the canoe men of the kingdom. They disliked the new Arab *régime*, and swore allegiance to Mwanga *en masse*. Mwanga built a fortified camp on one of the islands—Bulinguye. His power daily grew and increased. In spite of Stokes's advice, that he should make a dash on Kalema's capital, he preferred to wait, thinking, and possibly rightly, that Kalema would prove his own most deadly foe, and that in no short

time most of the people would return to their old
allegiance to himself. His position was a strong one,
and practically impregnable ; he held complete control
of the lake and was soon able, through his brave young
captain, Kagwa Apollo, to attack Kalema in earnest.
After several days of desperate fighting, with varying
fortune, the Christians at length proved victorious,
although they were far worse armed and fewer in
number than their foes. Kagwa stormed the royal
enclosure and took it and burnt it to the ground.
Kalema fled, followed by the conquering army, and the
pursuit was kept up for two days.   Kalema, however,
and his Arab friends made good their escape and
formed a strong camp upon the confines of Bunyoro ;
they had something like 1000 guns in their possession,
and afterwards proved a sore thorn in Mwanga's side.

After this success, Mwanga crossed over to the mainland. He had previously been joined by Walker and
Gordon and the French priests, the same devoted
missionaries whose adventuresome expulsion from
Buganda is related, pp. 267–270. This was a time of
great rejoicings among the Christian flock, and king
Mwanga was brought in triumph to the site of his new
enclosure, where he duly distributed—as he was forced
to do—the great chieftainships of the kingdom among
his faithful Christian keepers. Sebwato, mentioned on
p. 123 as Lugalama's captor, became ruler of the
province of Budu, and Kagwa, the brave young leader,
was made Katikiro or chancellor ; while 'Samweli,

faithful bringer in of tribute, received an important chieftainship called 'Mukamba.'

During the time that Mwanga was engaged in settling the country and building his royal enclosure, Kalema was not idle, and in spite of a great expedition sent against him, waxed so strong that Mwanga was forced to move his headquarters back to Bulinguye, his impregnable island. Things were now looking rather black when at this critical juncture the timely arrival of the vanguard of the Imperial East African Company's caravan, and the treaty concluded between Mwanga and his Christian chiefs on the one side, and the Company's agents on the other, again inclined the scale in favour of this puppet king.

And now the curtain must fall. Mujasi, the murderer, murdered; the chief judge, and many another heavy-handed oppressor, snatched away by violent, sometimes fearful deaths; Mwanga, after his flight and humiliation, left face to face with an implacable foe in the form of his last surviving brother—the two competing in doubtful warfare for the dangerous and slippery throne; Kalema a mere tool in the hands of treacherous Arabs, and Mwanga a pensioner on the favour of those very Christians whom he formerly persecuted. "We are herding Mwanga," writes one of them, "like an ox." How much of retribution four short years have seen, since that time when Mujasi received orders to seize the three first martyrs! Surely innocent blood cries from the ground, and an unseen hand righteously deals out their doom to evildoers!

CHAPTER XXII.

SECOND JOURNEY TO THE COAST.

WHILE the above stirring events were brewing in Buganda, I was far on my way to Zanzibar, having at the end of July, 1888, taken a sorrowful farewell of my best of friends Mackay, who had spared no pains to make my little caravan complete in every respect. We were rather more than a dozen, all told. My arms consisted of a Winchester repeating rifle, a revolver, and a Snider rifle, and three muzzle-loading guns. I had a fine big Unyamwezi donkey, of which, when I reached the neighbourhood of the Masai, those ignoble savages robbed me and left me to proceed on foot. However, I had the help of the donkey for the first five hundred miles of the march, which was an important consideration. I was by this time quite an old traveller, and I had in the boy Mwana awulira, whom I have before mentioned, an excellent interpreter, for he knew four African languages. He was also armour-bearer, as he carried my rifle, and combined this function with that of cook and general servant. Affectionate and as honest as the day, he was seldom tired and never out of temper. Add to this that he was my nurse when I was ill, and when I became blind my leader, it will be seen that if ransoming a slave be an act of charity, in this case I received an ample reward. I was far from well on the march, and was laid up six days at one village with bad fever. However, I struggled on to Ugogo, where I was attacked with ophthalmia. The prostration caused by frequent fevers had made me liable to this terrible complaint and to violent and prolonged toothache. The light caused me so much agony that I had to completely blindfold myself, and so in utter darkness for seven days I made the journey through Ugogo. Mwana awulira, the obedient child, did everything for me, and indeed all my followers were as kind as could be. They were mostly Wanyamwezi, and in spite of certain things which I could not but dislike about these people, they showed so many fine qualities that they won my sincerest admiration. Patience, fortitude, strong affection, dogged perseverance, were their better characteristics.

And so, in spite of the fact that I was blind and had toothache, I had a pleasant journey. As I neared Kisokwe, where I knew I should meet with a hearty welcome from the Coles, I found that constant want of sleep at night had so affected me that I could hardly walk straight; I seemed to be wandering in a circle and winding among awful abysses, down which I expected to fall. Riding the donkey made things worse. Sometimes I believed that I was walking round towards the right hand, at others to the left. I can hardly describe my sensation of relief when I heard the familiar voice of my kind-hearted host giving me a warm Irish welcome. He and his wife soon made me forget my past troubles, and among other kindnesses which he conferred, he drew my offending tooth.

Next day Dr. Pruen, the medical missionary from Kikombo, a new Mission station near Kisokwe, came over and examined my eyes. He pronounced the case a serious one, and said there was some danger of my losing my sight. He most kindly urged me to go back with him, saying he would like to have me near him, so that he could give me more frequent attention. I therefore returned to Kikombo with him, where for ten days I was most hospitably entertained by him and his wife. Soon after my arrival there, Dr. Pruen received a summons from Freretown to proceed at once to the coast, so the next few days were spent in packing. I sat most of the day with a shade over my eyes, and could do little more to help than by occasionally rocking the cradle ; for six weeks before a fine baby, little Stella, had made her appearance in this naughty and trouble-some world. Under any circumstances the journey for a young mother and six weeks old child would have been a trying and dangerous undertaking ; but ere we had half crossed the rocky mountains which led to Mamboya we received for the first time tidings of the terrible doings at Zanzibar, of the bombardment of Bagamoyo by the Germans, and the slaughter of many insurgents; this made things infinitely worse, and had not Mrs. Pruen been an exceptionally courageous woman I know not how we should have ever made the journey. The advice we received from Zanzibar was that we had better remain where we were, but at Kikombo there were hardly any stores, and at Mamboya there were no houses, and the rains were fast approaching. We decided that it was better to face the uncertain risk of the insurgents than the more certain peril of a wet season under insufficient shelter. We therefore sent letters to the coast at once asking that we might be informed if there was serious danger, and then went on quietly to Mamboya. The Pruens made their camp in the valley—they feared the cold of the mountain for the little one—while I took up my abode with my old friend Roscoe and his wife.

A fortnight passed and yet our messengers did not return, so notwithstanding my friends' hospitable invitation to remain with them, and in spite of their warnings of my indiscretion, I determined to go on and see for myself how matters stood. So bidding my companions farewell, I started again on the journey. I thought it would be better for me to be in front, as I should be able to send news back to the Pruens if there was really serious danger. Four days later, after crossing the beautiful rocky river of Mto ya mawe, we made our forenoon halt. I observed numbers of armed natives on the hill at the base of which the river flows. However, they made no impression on my mind, as I was intent on cooking. We were in a small village below the point where the warriors were gathered. The people at first were inclined to be un-friendly; but when I talked to them they thawed, and all went merry as a marriage bell. We soon left and went our way, but we had not gone far when messengers from Zanzibar came up; they were going to the Arab soldiers stationed on the other side of the river, and they so frightened my little band with the tidings which they brought that my men came and begged me not to go on until I had reliable news. The messengers told us, moreover, that our mail-men had been attacked near Zanzibar, and that one of them had been killed, because they were the white men's servants. We went on another mile or so and halted at Kwe Mazengo, a pretty village in the Nguru Hills. Next morning I sent off three of my men, armed with a couple of guns, carrying a letter to Bwana Heri, chief of Sadaani, and another to the British Consul at Zanzibar. I told my messengers I would remain till they returned; I was not sorry to wait here, for my boy Mwana awulira had become very ill with pleurisy or inflammation of the lungs, and could hardly crawl.

This was at the end of October 1888. The third day of my sojourn, a lad whom Dr. Pruen had dismissed arrived and told me that the Pruens had left Mamboya and were only a few marches behind. So I sent one of my men back to tell how I was detained at Kwa Mazengo waiting for news. A day or two later Pruen's caravan came in. He had also heard the story which my men had told me, that the warriors at the former village whom I

had seen had been holding a council with the intention
of killing me ; but eventually decided to leave me alone.
A night or two after my arrival at Kwa Mazengo, some
of the youths of the village were sitting out in the
moonlight, and I heard them talking in an insolent
manner about white men. I went out and said, "If
you have anything to say, come and say it here." They
slunk into their houses, but in a few days I had made
great friends with most of the village. Day after day
passed and our men did not return, and frequent reports
kept coming in of massacres of Europeans. Dr. Pruen's
porters were greatly frightened, and told him plainly that
if the Arabs made an attack, they could not help us;
but they would defend us against the "Washenzi" natives,
whom we did not fear. During the whole time I feared
our own Moslem porters more than all the natives put
together, and these men were daily becoming more
insolent as fresh reports of disasters to Europeans kept
coming in. Our case was a serious one, especially as
our cloth was running short. There was a French
Roman Catholic Mission some hours' distance, so we
wrote to the priests asking if they could let us have a
small supply ; and they most generously sent us two
pieces of thirty yards each, a great boon, as well as some
fruits and vegetables from their garden. We waited till
the 8th of November, and then determined to return to
Mamboya. When we had come within one long march
on our return journey to Mamboya our letters came in
from the coast ; this showed us that communication was

still open. We had, before leaving Kwa Mazengo, at
Mrs. Pruen's suggestion, written a tiny letter, which was
put in a needle-case as an envelope, and which we sent
off secretly by two trusty messengers, one of whom
concealed the minute missive about his person. We
had briefly explained our position, our shortness of cloth,
and the difficulties with the porters. The letters now
received showed that our messengers had not arrived
at Zanzibar, as there was no reference to them; but
Bwana Heri had sent one of his slaves to take our mail-
men through the insurgents, and he had succeeded in
doing so. The question now was whether, if we decided
to make the attempt to reach the coast, he could succeed
in passing us through as well. We were in a dilemma :
discomfort and starvation were frowning behind us at
Mamboya, fighting and tumult were looming before us
at the coast.

Mrs. Pruen had always been in favour of an advance,
and with many misgivings and questionings I went
across to their tent the day that our letters arrived to
say that I thought on the whole that this was the best
thing we could do. The chief point in favour of making
for the coast was that our porters were all willing and
ready for the journey, which they had previously refused.
So the next day we were once more walking towards
the sunrise. We made long forced marches ; Mrs. Pruen
was carried in the Bath-chair which Mrs. Hore has made
famous in her interesting book ' To the Tanganyika in
a Bath-chair ' ; it had been taken off the wheels, and

was carried slung on a pole resting on the shoulders of two men.

We went on without adventure till we reached a village some three marches from the coast. Here, while making a halt, suddenly we heard a great firing of guns outside the stockade, and up trotted the young half-bred Arab Abdallah on a fine Muscat donkey, followed by about twenty men. This was the fruit of Mrs. Pruen's needle-case letter. The messengers had taken it in safety to our energetic friend and agent, Mr. Muxworthy, at Zanzibar, who had handed it on to the Consul-General, Col. Euan-Smith. The latter went at once to the Sultan and prevailed upon him to send a peremptory order to the turbulent Abdallah, son of Bwana Heri, to go himself in person and escort us to the coast, which after some demur he proceeded to do. As we passed from village to village we could not but observe the scowling looks which greeted us; but by dint of talking and laughing with the people in a friendly way, the angry faces soon relaxed into smiles.

On Sunday, Nov. 18, we once more beheld the sea from Mkange. We were now at the most dangerous part of our journey, at the place where a missionary of the London Missionary Society, Mr. Brooks, lost his life a few weeks later. We had heard some time before that he was on his way to the coast. When he afterwards reached Mkange he acted just as I had done at Kwa Mazengo: sent some men on with a letter to Bwana Heri, chief at Sadaani, and awaited their return.

Some men came from Bwana Heri and walked into Brooks's camp when he was just on the point of returning towards Mamboya. One of these men came up and saluted him, and shook hands with him, saying, "Jambo Bwana?" "How do you do, sir?" at the same time another insurgent shot him dead from behind. He was the last of twelve English missionaries with whom I had been personally associated in some way or other who have lost their lives in Africa.

Before making our last march we received the unpleasant intelligence that the *Henry Wright*, the Mission steamer, had appeared off Sadaani; but that her boat had been fired on by the insurgents, and that the vessel had steamed back to Zanzibar.

Early on Monday morning, November 19th, 1888, we reached Sadaani; and as we entered the miserable place we saw every sign of preparation for fighting. The principal Arabs had sent their households inland for some miles, and nearly all the houses were stripped of their roofs. As we came into the town we discerned the portly figure of Bwana Heri coming to meet us with one or two other Arabs and large numbers of Indians who saluted us warmly. The chief greeted us with cold but studied politeness. The scowling mob through which we passed were silent. We were conducted to a filthy house, where we spent a long, uncomfortable day. Our porters were in great terror, and would not go anywhere far from where we were, except Mwana awulira, my faithful boy, who did not

U

understand politics, and walked with me through the town and down to the sea-shore, where he assured himself that the Nyanza here was really salt. We bought some eggs and then returned, but the hours dragged on wearily. We had to wait till midnight before we could go on board the miserable dhow which Bwana Heri had allowed us to hire. We tried in vain to sleep; I was lying on my bed outside in the verandah of the house, and could hear a constant stream of remarks, often with ugly words occurring in juxtaposition to the hated name Mzungu (white man). Before the time fixed for starting we made our way down to the sea by the soft light of the moon, and climbed into the dhow; she was lying over on her side, as the tide had not yet come in.

This was better than the stifling house and the half-understood insults of the insurgents, although we were in an extraordinarily uncomfortable position on the little poop deck, which was like the side of a house. Here we were reclining on the hard boards, watching with some uneasiness the Arab sentries armed with guns patrolling the beach. At last the whispering tide stole in and flowed around us, then gently rocked us, then lifted us up, and we were afloat. And soon the great lateen sail was hoisted, and we swept out to sea. But the faithless breeze failed as the light of day increased, and the cool of the morning gave place to the terrible blaze of the noontide sun; and so we lay " as idle as a painted ship upon a painted ocean."

Again the fickle breeze dallied with the sail and we

made some tardy progress. At last we sighted a ship approaching us, coming nearer and nearer—

> " Hither to work us weal;
> Without a breeze, without a tide, she steadies with upright keel."

It was the *Henry Wright* steamer, and so finally, at about 3 o'clock in the afternoon, after having been fifteen hours on the dhow, we went on board, and were soon clasping the hand of the kindly Scot, Captain Wilson, who commanded her.

I need not try and describe our feelings as the long strain of anxiety was suddenly removed; but I can describe how we revelled in toast and tea, and how our entertainer would insist on opening a bottle of champagne for our delectation. Strange it was to hear the steady thud of the engines as the little steamer flew through the water, and sadly I saw the Dark Continent die down on the horizon as Zanzibar came more clearly into view.

We were most kindly received by Colonel Euan-Smith, the able and courteous Consul-General. We could not but feel that his wise and prompt action had been the chief cause of our getting safely through the insurgents. The reaction prostrated us all with severe fever, and we met with the greatest attention from members of the Universities Mission, and I am sure that none of us will ever forget the kindness of the trained nurse who is one of the Mission staff. After more than a fortnight at Zanzibar I left for home, and reached England on Christmas Day, 1888.

THE END.

LONDON :

PRINTED BY WILLIAM CLOWES AND SONS, LIMITED,
STAMFORD STREET AND CHARING CROSS.

www.ingramcontent.com/pod-product-compliance
Lightning Source LLC
Chambersburg PA
CBHW020459270326
41926CB00008B/665